Attitude 3

The New Subversive Online Cartoonists

NANTIER · BEALL · MINOUSTCHINE
Publishing inc.
new york

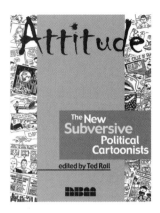
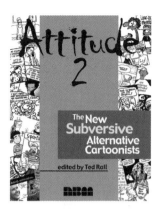

Also available:
ATTITUDE: The New Subversive Political Cartoonists, $13.95
ATTITUDE 2: The New Subversive Alternative Cartoonists, $13.95
ATTITUDE, featuring: Stephanie McMillan, $12.95
ATTITUDE, featuring: Neil Swaab, $10.95
ATTITUDE, featuring: Andy Singer, $10.95

Acknowledgments

To Terry Nantier of NBM Publishing, for encouraging this genre and helping to shine light on deserving artists. To J.P. Trostle, for the taste and discretion befitting a superb editor as much as an art director. Thank you to the contributing artists for their time and energy. I relied on the assistance and counsel of Ruben Bolling, Ted Keller, Maura McLaughlin, Mikhaela B. Reid, Martin Satryb, Cole Smithey, Ward Sutton, Kim Thompson, Tom Tomorrow, and others I'll be embarrassed to have omitted after press time. Love and thanks once again to my supportive and understanding family.

Editor: **Ted Rall**
Art Director: **J.P. Trostle**

We have over 200 titles; write
for our color catalog:
NBM
40 Exchange Place, Suite 1308
New York, NY 10005
see our web site at www.nbmpublishing.com
ISBN-10: 1-56163-465-4
ISBN-13: 978-1-56163-465-1

Library of Congress Cataloging-in-Publication Data

Attitude 3 : the new subversive alternative cartoonists / [edited by] Ted Rall.
    p. cm.
 ISBN 1-56163-465-4 (pbk. : alk. paper)
1. Cartoonists--United States--Interviews. 2. American wit and humor, Pictorial.
3. Comic books, strips, etc.--United States. 4. United States--Social life and
customs--Caricatures and cartoons. 5. United States--Politics and
government--Caricatures and cartoons. I. Rall, Ted.
II. Title: Attitude three. III. Title: New subversive alternative cartoonists.
 NC1305.A869 2006
 741.5'6973--dc22
                                    2006043247

Contents

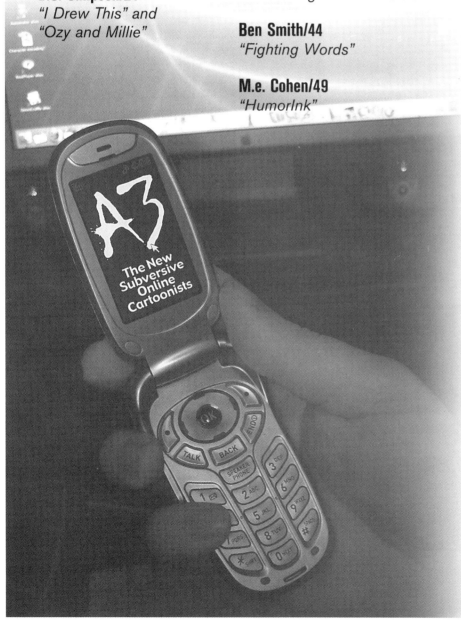

Eric Millikin

Foreword

Ted Rall tells you why webcomics are the Next Big Thing

In December 2005, a hundred political cartoonists submitted contributions to "Black Ink Monday," a one-day event organized by the Association of American Editorial Cartoonists, in order to protest the elimination of cartooning jobs at daily newspapers.

Although they're popular with readers, cartoonists argue, cartoons will go the way of the passenger pigeon unless someone is willing to pay for them to appear in print. "Guess they've never heard of the Internet," snapped "churchillbuff" on the right-wing Web site *Free Republic*.

Cartoonists are finding it increasingly difficult to get their work published in print. So what? What about the Web?

That's a standard response whenever someone points out that there are fewer print media outlets willing to pay for cartoons, whether controversial or tame. After all, the real estate of daily newspapers' comics sections is as rarefied as midtown

Steven Cloud

Richard Stevens

Thomas K. Dye

Manhattan's. New strips only get a shot at exposure after when older cartoonists die or retire, events that hardly ever happen thanks to two increasingly pervasive trends: successor cartoonists (neither "Hagar the Horrible," "Mary Worth," nor "Dennis the Menace" are drawn by their original creators), and reprints of classics ("Peanuts" and "Calvin & Hobbes" seem destined for such dubious immortality). And editorial pages are firing rather than hiring cartoonists. The rise of free alternative weekly newspapers like *SF Weekly* and *Miami New Times* during the Eighties and Nineties created openings

for cartoonists then locked out of the dailies, mostly to the benefit of cynical Generation Xers like Tom Tomorrow ("This Modern World"), Ruben Bolling ("Tom the Dancing Bug") and yours truly. Many of the beneficiaries of the alt-weekly boom became subjects of the first anthology in this *Attitude* series.

Now the weeklies are locked up too. A business model that opened markets as tiny as Wausau, Wisconsin, and Fayetteville, Arkansas, has expanded as far as it can go. And online classified advertising like Craigslist is killing the bottom lines of existing titles. Weekly readers are at least as loyal to their favorite comics as the geriatrics who peruse the dailies, making cancellations of existing features rare. So what is a bright, twentysomething Gen Y cartoonist to do to break into the business?

In 2000 cartoonist Scott McCloud published his controversial book *Reinventing Comics*, a dense follow-up to his 1993 *Understanding Comics* that argued that the future of comics is, as the aforementioned Free Republic guy posited, online. Key to webcomics as an economic model to support creators, McCloud predicted, would be the cre-

August J. Pollak

Adam Rust

ation of a culture of, and platform for, micropayments for online content. If a cartoonist could convince 10,000 readers to fork over a mere quarter each month, McCloud reasoned, a cartoonist could earn a reasonable base income from his or her work. Despite the ensuing dot-com crash, however, McCloud remained "convinced that the digital delivery of comics has the potential to revolutionize the industry, and that the aesthetic opportunities of digital comics are enormous."

After a number of false starts, a viable micropayment management system emerged in 2003. Nevertheless few webcartoonists, even those whose strips have proven popular, have been able to turn their work into a paying proposition. The exceptions tend to rely on ancillary merchandise such as T-shirts and buttons to keep their creditors at bay. But while webcomics remain a labor of love for the vast majority of professional cartoonists—I make this distinction in order to separate them from the vast hordes of amateurs producing work that may or may not eventually rise to that impossible-to-define level of quality that makes it possible to contemplate it as worthy of financial support—this book, which focuses on cartoonists whose work primarily appears online, testifies to the accuracy

Dale Beran and David Hellman

D.C. Simpson

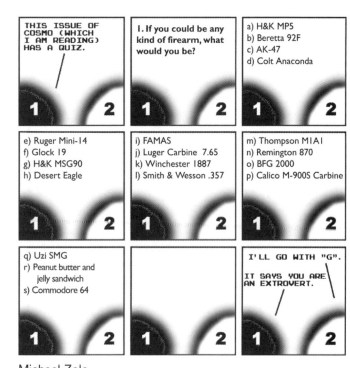

of McCloud's optimistic assessment of the form's potential as an art form.

"A Lesson is Learned But the Damage is Irreversible," a free-form painterly bit of mayhem by Dale Beran and David Hellman, would never have seen the light of a printing press had not the medium of webcomics removed such aesthetic limitations as traditional framing and narrative. Eric Millikin's "Fetus-X," one of the most interesting webcomics around, would have been dismissed after a passing glance by most newspaper and magazine editors—too sketchy, too highschooly, just too *too*. Mark Fiore makes political cartoons that do something that their print analogs never will: talk and move. And Michael Zole sends up the webcomics medium itself in "Death to the Extremist." Parody of the medium is the message, to garble ol' McLuhan.

Other *Attitude 3* cartoonists turned to webcomics because their work, which by design and appearance would have run in old-fashioned print a generation ago, couldn't find an outlet offline.

Michael Zole

Matt Bors

M.e. Cohen ("HumorInk") is a fairly traditional editorial cartoonist; Mark Poutenis ("Thinking Ape Blues") a commercially friendly artist whose work would fit in nicely in alternative weeklies (and, in one case, does). Others, like Nicholas Gurewitch ("Perry Bible Fellowship"), draw sustenance in equal parts from old and new media.

In some respects the world of webcomics, as visually and topically innovative and thrilling as it is, has some dismaying analogies to its print antecedent. Reflecting the webcomics from which they were chosen, only one of *Attitude 3's* twenty-one cartoonists is a woman. Almost all are white. If the print cartoonists profiled in volumes one and two enjoyed temporal diversity—with ages ranging from twenty to sixty-one—almost all of the current crop of webcomics creators are in their twenties to early thirties. Their work is anything but homogenous, but one can't help wondering whether their worldviews may be drawing from the same narrow gene pool of popular culture.

I've never subscribed to artistic affirmative action and this book reflects that. I cast a wide net to find these cartoonists and am convinced that they represent an exciting cross-section of a format of cartooning whose potential is only beginning to be explored. It's important to remember that, although all of these cartoonists are at least partly defined by their identities as Internet cartoonists, they're only working online because online is what there is at this particular moment in the development of media. They are cartoonists first, middle, and last —damned good ones, too.

Ted Rall

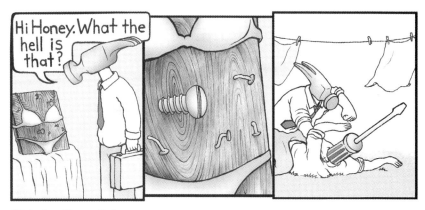

Nicholas Gurewitch

Ben Smith

Robert T. Balder

Jason Pultz

Minimalist expressionism through jagged dialogue

Jason Pultz, 29, is a Canadian-born (British Columbia) designer/illustrator for such clients as TVO Kids, Headgear animation, Cartoon Network, the Discovery Channel, Paramount parks, and Minute Maid. While at first his "Comic Strip" appears to fit neatly into the cut-and-paste school of Webcomics, his work surprises both in form and in content.

TED RALL: Is Scarybear you? Parts of you? Someone you know? Or no one in particular?

JASON PULTZ: Scarybear himself isn't really based on me or anyone specifically. I do believe that there are definitely parts of me in each character—one for each of my own traits. Naive scarybear. Pissed-off, oblivious Cowboy Rick. Knowledgeable Doggy and freak/outcast Birdboy, though they are pretty exaggerated versions of those traits. I think as an artist you can't help to put a bit of yourself in anything you create, especially your characters. It's what makes them seem real.

When I was deciding what kind of characters to make for my comic, aesthetically, I used a system of complementary opposites to figure out who good characters for my strip would be. Scarybear was first. What is the opposite of a large naive bear? An old Macintosh computer that wants to take over the world. Opposite of him? Why, a drunk cowboy, of course!

I thought there would be lots of dynamics to play with and tons of options to go in any direction I'd like. Sometimes I'll have an idea for a strip, and depending upon the theme—sad, pissed off rant, cute life observation—I'll use the corresponding character that suits the mood I'm in for that particular strip. They will be in fact the spokesperson for my message.

Lots of the stories/gags that come up in "Comic Strip" are in fact things that I or my friends have gone through. There are times where the lines that define each character are pretty blurry and it just seems like they are all alike and they are basically just really mean to each other.

Are you Canadians mean? We Americans think of Canadians as calm and often drunk. We look to the Aussies for nastiness.

Aussies aren't mean, they're rowdy. We Canadian men hate them and their sexy accents. They come over here and seduce our women with that shit. I think Canadians can be really mean. I think we are a calm, easy-going bunch. Until you piss us off. It takes a lot to get us angry. But once you do—watch out.

What's the difference between Canadian and American comics?

I am personally influenced by lots of work coming from the U.S.: artists like [Dan] Clowes, [Chris] Ware, [Charles] Burns. I think there is some really great stuff coming out of Canada. There is lots of talent here. I think a big part of that is the climate.

You have little pockets in Canada, like Winnipeg, that during the winter months are almost uninhabitable. So what happens is that young people end up moving there because it's super cheap. (You can rent a house there for about the same price of renting a one-bedroom here in Vancouver.) Summers in Winnipeg are warm, winter hits and then everyone starts to hibernate. They have this pent-up energy and they start drawing, painting and recording songs. You have a city of people doing that for half the year, you are gonna get some interesting stuff.

Reminds me of when I lived in Ohio.

Vancouver has kind of the opposite problem. The weather here is so nice, people are out on the beach or up skiing and snowboarding. Not much work is getting done. Nowadays you really need to think worldwide. Because of the Internet and how easy it is to put up a webcomic (good or bad) you are directly on the same level as everyone else out there. I read some amazing French comics, great German comics. It's to the point where I'm not even sure where the stuff I'm reading comes from. Between the ease of posting to the Web, wider print distribution and books being translated into every possible language, it really comes down to the work itself instead of where it's coming from.

Your work employs a clean, minimal style. Do you use a computer or regular pencil to draw?

I try to make my comics as clear as possible. It's really about the joke, or story I'm trying to tell. To do that successfully in the limited space of four or so panels I don't think you need lavish backgrounds and lots of detail. I see comics all the time that have panels cramped to the ceiling with super-detailed drawings, elaborate word balloon systems and fancy fonts. It's so busy, not only does it take away from your story, it just becomes unreadable and defeats the purpose in the beginning. My eyes just blur it all together.

I draw everything by hand, ink it and scan it in. I use a program to convert the drawings to vector images and then color and lay them out in Illustrator. I have a

Jason and the future policewomen.

cut-and-paste style. I have a library in Illustrator of all of my characters and their many poses, ready to be dropped into comic panels with hilarious results!

One of the main reasons why I choose to do my comic in the cut-and-paste style has been because I'm very slow at drawing comics. If I did a comic where I drew every panel out I would have made maybe two comics and would have quit about four years ago. Instead I have this cut-and-paste system and I've made close to three hundred comics. It's what works for me.

I have however gotten a lot of flack from other comic artists and fans that hate this type of comic.

Really? What feedback you've received about your comic?

I got a few saying how they think my writing is good but hate how I just have the same characters cut-and-pasted here and there. Again I think it's about the story. Yes, there are the more conventional comic methods, but there are so many comics that are just frames that repeat but you don't even notice because the jokes are so funny. My comics can be pretty crass sometimes and aren't for everyone. My girlfriend says I'm a soft guy that makes a hard comic. But ninety-nine percent of the feedback I get is totally positive. These letters are the main reason why I've kept making "Comic Strip" for so long.

I've received e-mails from high school kids in Italy who say their town sucks and they read my comic to pass time. I've received an e-mail from a sixty-year-old lady who had forwarded some of my pretty racy comics about dating and sex to her sixty-three-year-old friend to help her get back into the dating scene at such an old age. I got an e-mail from the zinc miners of Canada. Every day the office secretary would fax my latest strip down into the mine as motivation for these guys who are busting their asses.

It blows my mind that people even read my comics, let alone look forward to them. I just want to make people laugh. Make them laugh out loud. It's pretty hit or miss, but when you get it, it's totally worth it.

Has "Comic Strip" made the move from the web into the world of print? Is that something you'd be interested in? Do you see any benefits from that?

From the very start I had designed my comic to be print-friendly. That's why it's black-and-white to begin with. My goal has always been to eventually make a book. The scary thing about print is that it's so permanent compared to the Web. On the Web if you make a mistake, delete, redo, upload. It's cheap, visible and changeable. Print is expensive, limited and permanent. Just putting my first book together has been like learning a new language. I'm so used to the World Wide Web but now I need to learn about margin size and binding.

Just recently, for a period of six months or so, I have had the fortune of having "Comic Strip" syndicated in three major Canadian cities in a major free daily newspaper. For any cartoonist, especially a web cartoonist, it was like hitting a jackpot.

My comic was now being read by millions all over Canada. It was pretty surreal. I'd be in a Denny's with my brother all nervous because across at the next table was some old woman just finishing up the last article and heading to the crossword/comics page. "Oh God! She is gonna hate my comic!"

Jason and a rabbit in a photo shoot from Jason's art school short film "Bad Flake."

Jason playing guitar for his surf band The Pauls.

It was a mind-blowing experience to know that you couldn't walk ten paces down the street without bumping into one of these boxes. These little green boxes on every street corner, each of them holding one of my comics! Every day! The benefits of this were pretty great, tons of positive letters and actually receiving checks for making my weird little comics! Made it seem so legit.

The downsides were there too—fielding calls from the autistic society of Canada demanding an explanation why I'm making fun of handicapped people. Good times.

(P.S. My younger brother is autistic and probably my number one fan!)

Many webcomic artists end up drawing themselves into their own comics. Why did you decide to do it? Vanity? Is Scarybear not enough—do you want the spotlight on Jason Pultz?

I think it's best when artists do work based on what they know. It seems real and natural. The subject everyone is an expert on is themselves. I always thought it would be funny to put myself in the comic. Just to show the audience a little more about me. Make my other characters seem as real to the audience as they do to me.

A big part of putting myself in the comic has been story matter. At the time all that was going on in my mind had been my health. My life came to a halt. I moved across the country back home to my family because I was slowly deteriorating. I was diagnosed with a few scary things one of them being Crohns' disease. Part of me dealing with being sick has been to vent my life into my comics. I try to still make the comics funny in light of the subject matter. It was/is a way for me to cope.

One unexpected result of this has been feedback—not only people sending me info on new therapies or medications—but also lots of people, that because of these comics, and the similarities in how they felt to what I was describing in my comics, went to their doctors and got checked out. I would literally be diagnosing my readers.

Richard Stevens

Girl dates robot. See what happens.

Richard Stevens' hugely popular "Diesel Sweeties," a tender tale of interaction and apparent romance between a sentient robot and an ex-porn star, began in 2000. According to his official biography, Stevens "often lose[s] titanic battles with his cat" and is "possibly the most inappropriate college professor ever." You can take a test to determine which "Diesel Sweeties" character you are most similar to at http://home.mn.rr.com/couplandesque/quizzes/sweeties.htm.

TED RALL: How and why did you develop "Diesel Sweeties'" pixelated art style?

RICHARD STEVENS: The art style was kind of an accident. It was a couple of years after college and I had a full-time job that I absolutely hated. I had one of those little revelations in my head that I should sit down and make a comic because I could afford to do so for the first time in my life. I'd kind of stopped making comics because I was studying graphic design and that ate up most of my time. I gave myself a deadline to come up with an art style and make pages for a very simple concept: girl dates robot.

After a month of messing around with very uninspired ink work and etching-style drawings in Illustrator, I just started fumbling around with making icons in Photoshop. I'd done some pixelated-looking projects for some album covers in my school portfolio and one thing just led to another. I scrapped the first few strips I'd done, pared it all down to pixels and had something I was actually happy to show people for the first time since I was a little kid. The fact that the computer art was nostalgic and a good fit for the content was a huge bonus.

After meeting many of my colleagues, my wife says that cartoonists always draw themselves as a central character in their work. Are you the robot?

I'm only Clango on my good days. I pretty much identify with all the main characters at one point or another in my week. On the bad days, it's the pissed-off Red Robot. When I'm overdoing the caffeine and weird stimulants from the health food store, it's Maura the drunk ex-porn star. When I catch myself hating things just because someone I don't like enjoys them, it's Indie Rock Pete.

I wish I could honestly say the strip was my viewpoint filtered through a main char-acter. I think that because of the stripped-down style, I had to originally go with characters I could sum up in one line. This led to the strip as a whole being an extremely loose diary, just not from any singular perspective. This gives me a lot of leeway when people think I am writing personal stuff—I'm the only one who knows which side of the issue I actually stand on.

Do your characters provide a blank template you can use to superimpose what-

ever you happen to be thinking about at a given time?

That pretty much sums it up. I sit down with whatever is in my head that day and pick the characters who fit the points of view I need to make the joke work. I think that writing comics is only "hard" if you don't know your characters or you're trying to please an editor. Lately, I'm getting even crazier about this stuff and waiting until nighttime to make a comic for midnight, treating it more like improv or stand-up. Sometimes that means I'm up until four in the morning writing fifty new slogans for every state in America, but the readers seem to dig it more when it's fresher. I guess life really is a bowl of cherries. Insert sex joke here.

I do my best cartoons—well, the cartoons that readers like best—on deadline. I tend to overthink when I have too much time. Then everything gets convoluted.

Deadline is the best thing ever. That's why I get mad at "professional" webcartoonists who fuck off on deadlines.

Most of your work falls into the "talking head" category—people talking to each other, exchanging glib witticisms. Is this a

conscious choice or would you consider other formats—fake ads, trippy dream sequences, deconstructed what-have-you?

Call me guilty of just loving dialogue! I'd love to do more visual stuff on a more frequent basis but it doesn't always fit in with the style of this comic. The funny thing is that when I do something along the lines of what you're suggesting, I get a lot of really happy e-mail. Maybe I should do more of that stuff? One of my favorite comics I ever did involved a dream sequence starring the Kool-Aid Man, one of my childhood heroes and someone who is directly responsible for many of my political beliefs.

Are you aware of how most "deconstruction" is done in webcomics? I try to avoid "deconstruction" in webcomics because when it's done, it's done very poorly. In paper comics, you'll see these huge deconstructionist stories like "Watchmen," where someone takes very well-established structures and history and then turns them on their head in a clever way. We don't really have that on the Web yet. Most of the deconstructionist things I've seen are strips by some goofball who thinks that breaking the fourth wall is the greatest thing since [the font] Comic Sans.

How most comic strips begin on the Internet:

Panel one: "Hello! We are the main characters."

Panel two: "Boy, I hope we are not supposed to be funny. I have not had my insert-carbonated-drink-here yet today."

Panel three: "I don't have any ideas here. I need to go play XBOX."

Panel four: "OMG! See you tomorrow, the comic is over."

After you read about five thousand comic strips that begin like that, you really appreciate the ones who don't and you do your very best to maintain suspension of disbelief with your characters.

Would "Diesel Sweeties" work as well in the print form?

Sometimes it does, sometimes it doesn't. I've made books of new material and reprints that looked good to me, but I'd never give up the ability to just publish insane amounts of comics for free on the Internet. People who are really into the strips enjoy the books. I really need to get my ass in gear and get more stuff in print. If I don't, it will be like I never existed as soon as all the computers explode. Note to al Qaeda: Please wait until I do back-ups!

What are some pros and cons of web vs. print?

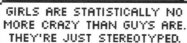

I personally prefer the insanely bright color possibilities on the screen as opposed to the printed page. Working online also gives me the ability to work right on deadline and to make revisions when I goof. It's also great to be able to just expand a comic by a couple of panels if I want to make an extra joke or two.

Printed books are more of an intimidating, magic place for me. There are so many little quality things you can do on a printed page that don't work on the Internet, and that's not even considering their permanence! I like comic books so much that it's kind of scary when I have to put something on actual paper. I think that's part of why I do Web stuff—that weird psychological barrier I've had since age three isn't there.

Do you see yourself doing this exact same strip for the foreseeable future?

I don't see myself quitting any time soon. I like being there every day for people. The routine is simultaneously relaxing and really good for my productivity. As far as different comics go, my goal would be to get caught up and fast enough to do an extra strip or two and add those to my day. It always annoys me when people just throw their hands up in the air and cancel a popular comic or quit a band that people love. I don't think that an artist really "owes" people a certain amount of work, but I also don't see the point of selfishly denying thousands of people something that might make their day a little easier.

I don't really have a big story I'm telling, so I don't see the point of quitting until it just "isn't in me any more." I figure I have at least another thousand of these comics in me, even though it will probably be a completely different strip by the time I get there. I'm just gonna pull them out of my head one at a time until I start getting a lot of e-mail telling me that I stink.

Comic strips are a funny thing—in comic books, your first issue typically sells best. In movies, you can get a couple sequels out before people get sick of you. In a strip, you're in the awesome position of being there as a constant in peoples' lives—and as such, you grow slowly for years and years at a time. I think that's rad. Why would anyone give that up?

D.C. Simpson

Two works that avoid the ossified print comic strip paradigm

Some comic strips are drawn by two people; some cartoonists draw two strips. D.C. Simpson is the creator of "I Drew This" and "Ozy and Millie," both of which appear in *Funny Times* and "a smattering of daily and weekly papers, assorted Web sites (most of which don't pay)." Twice a finalist for the Scripps-Howard Charles M. Schulz College Cartoonist Award, Simpson will only specify that he's in his mid-twenties. "I like to be kind of vague about it in preparation for when I'm old," he explains.

TED RALL: You draw two strips: "I Drew This" and "Ozy and Millie." Please explain the differences between the two. Why do you feel the need for separate creative outlets?

D.C. SIMPSON: "Ozy and Millie" is a lot older. I started it when I was an undergrad, and Millie was a character I'd been drawing in sketchbooks for at least five years in one form or another even at that point. At the time it was something I started doing as an experiment—like "hey, I've always loved comic strips, let's try and draw one." I was reading a lot of "Calvin & Hobbes," a lot of

"Bloom County"—you know, the same two influences that literally every cartoonist my age cites. I think I ripped them both off a lot in the early going. Then I stuck it up on the Web because it was a convenient place to get instant feedback. I had this idea from early on that I was grooming it for syndication, although it hasn't really worked out that way. I never intended at the time to become an Internet cartoonist; in 1998 the idea existed, but only barely, and it wasn't the massive thing it is now. I think that makes me kind of old school.

"I Drew This" appeared later, in grad school, but by then I'd been experimenting

on the side with political cartoons for several years. It wasn't so much that I decided I needed a second outlet as just that I walked into the university newspaper office and said "I draw cartoons and I understand you need people" and accidentally volunteered that I could draw political cartoons. The editor said, "Oh, good, we need some" and I went "okay" and then I walked out thinking: "You idiot, you just volunteered yourself into extra work. You could have sold them 'Ozy and Millie' and gotten the exact same amount of money for no additional work."

These days, though, I'm glad I have two outlets, because I used to have to cram everything I was thinking into "Ozy and Millie," so in the beginning it was kind of this weird hybrid. One week I'd be writing about kids getting bullied in school and then I'd be talking about the Clinton impeachment. I don't think specific political stuff works so well in "Ozy and Millie"

PEOPLE FROM MASSACHUSETTS AIN'T AS **AMERICAN** AS US SOUTHERNERS.

WE'RE **WAY** MORE PATRIOTIC THAN TRAITOROUS BLUE-STATE ELITISTS.

SO THEN WHAT'S WITH THE T-SHIRT CELEBRATING THE TIME YOU ATTEMPTED ARMED SECESSION?

SHUT UP, HIPPIE.

because I have existing characters to work with and I don't want to make them mouthpieces for me. I like to do more allegorical political stuff, sort of "Pogo"-esque stuff, because that way I can work with the characters' existing personalities. "I Drew This" gives me an outlet if I want to, say, get wonky about health care or Iraq; I think that by giving me an outlet for the specific political stuff, it's made "Ozy and Millie" a stronger strip because I'm no longer trying to cram in things that don't quite fit.

Very broadly, "I Drew This" is about what I think, and "Ozy and Millie" is about how I feel. Very broadly.

What prompted you to give up hope of landing a syndication deal for "Ozy and Millie"?

I had submitted it about eight times and I kept getting rejected by everyone. I might try again one of these days, but for some reason syndicates don't seem to think they can sell it. Their loss.

Things change. What doesn't fit a syndicate's needs one month might be per-

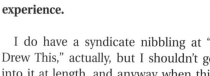

fect for them the next. I know from experience.

I do have a syndicate nibbling at "I Drew This," actually, but I shouldn't go into it at length, and anyway when this

actually gets published the situation will probably be different. So...the strip I tried to groom for syndication? No go. The strip where I just shoot my mouth off? Apparently marketable. I don't understand any of this.

Neither do I. I get gigs I don't deserve and passed over for stuff for which I think I'm a natural. Go figure.

I'm coming to the conclusion that that's pretty much a universal. Every cartoonist I know has a story about just tossing off some cartoon on a deadline, thinking it's the worst thing they've ever done, and it ends up being the most popular cartoon they've ever put out.

Absolutely. Meanwhile their favorite strip of all time lands like a wet towel.

It was a long time before I learned to stop being angry when people didn't get things I wrote. I was way more attached to each individual cartoon, when I was starting out. Each one was like one of my children. Now I've done thousands of them and no one cartoon stands out for me. They all just kind of blend together into a single body of work, and if people don't get today's I just move on to tomorrow's.

Animal characters are cartoon syndication crack, right?

You know, I've spent years trying to figure out what it is with syndicates and animal characters. "Ozy and Millie" seem supremely marketable to me. But I've actually been told that can work against you. I've been told "syndicates are wary of animal strips because people get too attached to the characters and it's hard to get rid of them." I've heard it put that way by more than one person. And it makes less than zero sense to me. It's like saying "oh, our store doesn't stock that product, too many people wanted to

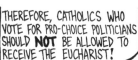

buy it." There has to be some part of that explanation I'm not grasping.

"I Drew This" features a bald eagle wearing a beret. Please explain yourself to the freedom-fries contingent reading this.

Okay. To all the right-wing French haters reading this: Joe Eagle wears that beret specifically to piss you off.

Really?

Pretty much. After 9/11 I actually had an American flag pin on my jacket for a while because it felt like, for the first time in my politically aware life, the flag belonged to all of us, not just to wingnuts. And then some time during the run-up to the war in Iraq, they stole it back and I had to take the pin off again. So when I created Joe, it was like "okay, I'm going to take another American symbol and associate it as closely with things I know you hate as I can." It seemed funny at the time.

The formats you use for each strip are very traditional: horizontal comic strip for the character-driven humor of "Ozy and Millie" and the black-and-white editorial cartoon format for "I Drew This." You're on the Web now. Why adhere to traditional print formats?

Because I'm used to it. I really don't have a better reason than that. Also both strips appear in print at least somewhere so there's something to be said for sticking to a single format even if it's a little arbitrary at this point. I know people who do strips that don't run at a consistent size and putting together their book collections is a lot more work.

I suppose if I woke up tomorrow thinking, "you know, I'd be able to do much better work at a different size" I'd feel perfectly free to switch. But it's never happened, so I just kept doing what I was used to.

Ah, momentum! The key to successful warfare. Or inertia.

When Bill Watterson switched to doing his "Calvin & Hobbes" Sunday strips at a larger, much more free-form size, it started taking him what, two or three times as long to get them done? And I'm a fundamentally lazy person. I don't have any grand ambition to create museum-quality works of stunning visual composition, though I think the world of cartoonists who do. I just have stories to tell and stuff to rant about. In my case, having a stock format keeps me from getting distracted.

What do you offer to the world of cartooning that you see missing in other artists' work?

By its very nature, the question sort of implies that I became a cartoonist at least in part because I thought the world of cartooning fundamentally lacked something that I could offer it, which I should say upfront isn't the case. It just sounded a lot more fun than learning how to do something, you know, of actual value. That said, I think there are a few things that make me stand out, at least in small ways.

In the case of "Ozy and Millie," I think I write from the standpoint of some-

Simpson on the road recently, visiting some of America's landmarks. So to speak.

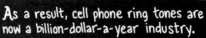

one who as a kid was very different—if you put the two title characters together you get a sort of self-portrait. I was the weird kid wrestling with whether life had meaning and whether free will existed and was much too busy with that to play flag football. And I think strips about childhood and adolescence are mostly either about cool kids, the kind I hated and still hate, or else not really about kids at all—I think a lot of them present children as sort of idealized cute puppets who exist purely for adult amusement. I think that speaks to some people. I think people who were that way as kids and are still that way as adults feel kind of under-represented.

As far as IDT goes, I don't see a lot of people presenting the political as personal. There are very personal strips that chronicle the author's life, and there are very political cartoons, but I think IDT is a kind of unique blend—I tell readers what I think about political issues, but in the end it's about my reaction almost more than about the actual issue. Sometimes I'll just up and drop politics for the day and illustrate some story from my childhood or something that happened to me when I was at the store, because to me the political and the personal can't be separated so easily. I'm only writing about it in the first place because I get angry or sad.

If you won the lottery, would you still draw cartoons?

Of course, and they wouldn't change at all. Except that I'd buy new brushes more often, so the line quality would be better.

Brian McFadden

No large sea creatures, no Moby Dick, not even cetaceans

Googling "Brian McFadden" yields fan sites for the former member of the British pop band Westlife. The British singer and the American cartoonist are two different guys, however, and the latter wants you to know that the former "blows." McFadden (the cartoonist) is 26, from Massachusetts, and fairly self-deprecating even by cartooning standards: his official biography notes that "Big Fat Whale" was "terrible, even by webcomic standards." Eventually, he continues, "it continued to overcome mediocrity and eventually abandoned the character that gave the strip its name." Contrary to McFadden's protestations, however, his work has been amusing and interesting for some time. Clevelanders can read BFW in the *Free Times*.

TED RALL: If and when you pitch "Big Fat Whale" to an editor, how do you describe it? What genre of comics does it fit into?

BRIAN McFADDEN: I've just started the process of putting together a second promotional package to send out to the edi-

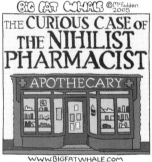

tors of alt-weeklies. I describe it as sketch comedy in comic strip form. I'm not sure if that's accurate, but I think it's a decent hook for a pitch.

You alternate between political topics and observational humor. Is that intentional?

Sometimes. If I notice I'm starting to get three political comics in a row, I try to throw something together for the folks who enjoy humor, but have no idea what's going on in the world. The uninformed masses are a bloc I shamelessly try to appeal to.

I detect the influence of Ruben Bolling's "Tom the Dancing Bug" [*Attitude*] in your work. Am I wrong?

Nope. I didn't start reading alternative comics until college, and he was one of the comics carried by the *Baltimore City*

Paper. After reading him for a couple years, I realized I could do a comic about whatever I wanted instead of being stuck to a particular set of characters or whatever was dominating the news cycle at the time.

So few cartoonists seem to realize that the only rules are those they impose on themselves.

That's not always a bad thing. It gives them structure and their audiences something to become attached to. I'm out there in the wilderness, trying to put new crap together every week.

But some artists start to believe that their own, or older cartoonists', stylistic rules and precedents are inherent rather than wholly arbitrary.

I see. When I was starting out, I wasn't skilled enough to come up with something that was my look, so I just tried to illustrate the jokes I had written and write lettering that was legible, something I'm still struggling with today.

How does your family react to "Big Fat Whale"?

My parents are extremely supportive, and they have similar politics, but they don't "get" the jokes. They're more of a Robin Williams and Carrot Top crowd.

Oh, come on. There is no Carrot Top "crowd."

There is. That guy's rich. He sells out everywhere. They're like the people who came out in droves to see "The Passion of the Christ." I never met any of them anywhere, but there they were, millions of them.

You're scaring me. Does the strip support you financially?

Sort of. I'm still mooching of my parents, so my expenses are limited. I don't have a top hat and a monocle, or health insurance.

Don't be jealous of the Monopoly man. You'd have to squint all day to hold the

eyepiece in. And, without health insurance, you're motivated to stay in shape! What medium—the Web, alternative weeklies, dailies, magazines, something else—do you hope to see become a paying venue for your work?

I would've never guessed you'd show me the bright side of our horrible health care system. I suppose alt-weeklies would be the best fit but for some reason they only run a couple of comics each. And with all the extremely talented established cartoonists they run, I don't see why they'd take on an unknown. My goal is just to get my name out there as a person who is capable of being funny and using that to get someone to read my scripted work. It has been a lifelong dream of mine to sell out and move to Los Angeles and write crappy jokes for sitcoms.

Actually, mine too. But I don't have the foggiest on how I would start, and the thought of starving to death under the blazing L.A. sun depresses me even more than starving to death on a park bench in Manhattan. So, is there a prehistory to BFW: i.e., earlier strips?

Not really. When I was eight I had one called DAP which was a ripoff of Garfield. Then I just doodled for a dozen years until I started BFW. The strip itself has changed a lot over the years. It started out about a surly whale and his friend a

A random shot of McFadden from his suburban childhood. From 1987, when he was 7 years old.

Brian McFadden

Nope, he didn't meet Reagan—this was a novelty photo taken at a New England amusement park in 1988.

molesting squid. It's essentially a different strip now. I was just too cheap to buy a different domain.

So if the weeklies are locked up—and with declining ad revenues, they're shrinking—will the Magical World Wide Web become a venue where cartoonists like you can make a living as well as express themselves?

I hope so, but I have no idea. The business end of cartoons is something I'm completely unskilled with. I know subscription services have had some success, and maybe micropayments are an option, but people have spent the past decade convincing themselves that everything on the internet should be free. I think the only hope is a better advertising model than the intrusive pop ups and flash games that irritate everyone. My one idea was something like BlogAds, but for webcomics. I was too lazy to follow up on it though.

What are BlogAds?

They allow advertisers to buy a block of advertising on a bunch of different sites, some they've never heard of, but all reach a similar demographic. They run on Tom Tomorrow's ["This Modern World," *Attitude*] site.

For the time being, then, you're saying that you continue to draw the strip from a state of fiscal hopelessness? If nothing changes, will you keep doing it?

Not indefinitely. I'm twenty-six and I can't stomach the thought of being a starving artist in my thirties. So barring wooing some heiress, I'll suck it up and eventually take some engineering job. I'd still do the comic, but I wouldn't be able to guarantee a new one every week. Working at jobs I don't like drains the funny from my brain.

I'd like to say, by the way, that "The Day the Earth Got Its Groove Back" made me laugh harder the third time I read than the second time, at which time I found it still funnier than the first.

Thanks. I have no musical ability, but the state of radio is really aggravating. I have to hunt down college radio to hear anything new.

That's as it has always been, but take it from an over-forty guy: enjoy your musical youth. Now I walk into CD stores and have no idea what genre most music is, much less whether or not I'd like it. It's like shopping in a foreign country where you can't read the language.

I think I've become a musical old man before my time. I think most of the stuff out there is garbage.

If you could wish away the existence of any single currently living human being, whom would you choose to disappear?

That's a trick question, because if I say Bush, that puts Cheney in office. I'll have to go with Larry the Cable Guy.

Alas, poor Lawrence!

A young McFadden preparing for the life of an editorial cartoonist.

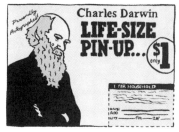

Matt Bors

Skewering sacred cows with punk rock glee

At 23 a recent graduate of the Art Institute of Pittsburgh, Matt Bors joins a proud tradition of such brilliant Ohio political cartoonists as Mike Peters, Milt Priggee and, um, you know. His fierce attack on left and right alike, "Idiot Box," runs in *Seven Days, the Buffalo Beast, Funny Times, the Free Press*, and campusprogress.org.

TED RALL: Did you name your strip after the argot for television, as a takeoff on the panel format of cartoons, or something else?

MATT BORS: Well, both television and a takeoff of the cartoon format. Around the time I started the strip I was also cutting TV out of my life. I look at television as one of the worst aspects of our culture. The news is terrible, the shows are a terrible, it's nauseating. I also thought it played well with there being boxes/panels and the comic often contains many idiots we call our leaders.

A lot of people swear off TV, but can't stick

with it. Could you? Aren't you depriving yourself of a valuable source of parody material?

I watched absolutely zero TV for my last year of college and since then I've watched very little. It definitely is great source material for comics and political commentary, so I do watch some. I'll turn on MTV or Fox propaganda while I'm eating just to get myself worked up over whatever is on. I figure if I multitask and only watch it when I'm doing something else like eating, it's not as big a waste of time. If I had to do without it for the rest of my life, it wouldn't be hard. I have so much I like to do with the small amount

of free time I have that TV just isn't anywhere on my radar. I need to be aware of what folks like [Fox News hosts Bill] O'Reilly and [Sean] Hannity are puking out everyday, but now there are blogs that watch TV for me and post all the must-see ridiculousness.

Do you rely on blogs as a primary news source?

I wouldn't say I have a primary news source. I read newspapers, magazines, listen to NPR and Air America, and check out the blogosphere. I'm a news junkie, which is mandatory for doing a weekly political cartoon.

I should probably go about finding how to write all my subscriptions off as part of my freelance research. I might save some.

I'm not an accountant, but my accountant says it's OK.

This is my first year really getting paid for freelance comics and illustration so I'm trying to figure out how to file and write off all my supplies and whatnot.

What kind of stories make you sit up and think to yourself that they might make good fodder for "Idiot Box"?

I'm a big fan of the completely absurd aspects of stories we hear every day. Usually politics in this country is already stretched to the limits of human comprehension and believability so it's becoming harder and harder to exaggerate things. We are talking about a country that has a serious political debate about whether or not someone intentionally "splashed" urine on a Koran [at Guantánamo Bay, as reported by *Time*], while the larger picture of why we are holding people in detention camps in Cuba without being charged with crimes goes largely unnoticed. Why does this place exist? Do people wonder what is going on in Cuba?

I'm a big fan of a strip Lloyd Dangle ["Troubletown," *Attitude*] did in which he stopped in the middle of the comic and declared from his drawing table that reality had surpassed his ability to make satire of it.

What's even more horrifying about the Koran-splashing incident at Guantánamo is the military's "defense": According to the Department of Defense, a soldier was urinating on a prisoner. His urine "accidentally" splashed onto the Koran.

See Ted, we aren't intentionally mistreating the Koran. Hey, know why [the inmates] have one? Because we are nice enough to supply them with it! They should be grateful. The piss probably got on the book because he put his hands up or something. Should've just taken it like a man.

Were you at all graphically influenced by derf ["The City," *Attitude*]?

I've seen his stuff since I live near Cleveland, but no. I wasn't aware of too many "alternative" artists until I read the first *Attitude* book, to tell you the truth. The person who really got

me excited about this kind of stuff was Shannon Wheeler ["Too Much Coffee Man," *Attitude 2*]. I found out about his

strip and just fell in love with the cynicism.

From there I picked up on you and

Bors' illustration for the Miami New Times

Tom Tomorrow ["This Modern World"] which led me to *Attitude*. I'm not sure I'm graphically influenced by anyone in particular with my cartooning style. I've always been into drawing more realistic comics until a few years ago when I started political strips. It was really hard parsing down my style, trying to get something that looked good in a strip format. I'm still evolving in that respect.

Does the Web present a different set of presentational challenges than print?

It's different, but I don't think there are too many challenges. You see the final product on your screen before anyone else so you can tweak to your liking. I suppose if you don't know how to work graphics or web programs it could be really difficult. In print there are so many factors that can screw up you work I think it's more challenging.

What's the best reaction you've ever gotten to a cartoon? The worst?

I've can't say I've had too many experiences in person with readers so it would have to be e-mail I've got. I've got random hate mail before, some vicious stuff from people. Nothing too bad, but I wouldn't want to make some asshole's day by referring to a specific incident in print.

The best reaction would be editor

calling out of the blue and saying they stumbled across my stuff on the net and want to run it. It happened yesterday with the Buffalo Beast. Another time someone said they liked a strip of mine and it inspired them to do a comic that they got into a magazine, so that felt good.

The worst is when you can't get a reaction because your cartoon won't be printed. In the student paper at my

college a new editor would leave out some of my strips. I knew she was very Christian and the ones that never saw print had to do with abortion or euthanasia or something. She would never say the real reason, just that there wasn't enough space that week, but I knew. Oh, I knew.

What is your primary goal as a cartoonist? To entertain? To inform?

No, getting laid. But other than all the money and women it's just to make people laugh at this whole big shit-storm we're a part of. Maybe someone can look at a situation in a new way or find out something they didn't know before, but I don't know how much actual effect cartooning has on things. I know it's cathartic for me. I have to draw comics.

Has "Idiot Box" gotten you laid?

:'(no. I might hang up the pen soon as a result.

That's sad. My cartoons got me laid, and that was back in college when I sucked even more than I do now. Which brings us to our last question: Is self-loathing a standard-issue character trait for cartoonists?

I don't self-loathe, I self-love. At least once a day.

Maybe that's the answer.

David Hellman & Dale Beran

Two friends collaborate on a painterly hell ride through the depraved depths of youthful imagination

"A Lesson Is Learned But The Damage is Irreversible" explores the limits of pessimism and fatal consequence in a universe that would be difficult to imagine on the printed page. Baltimore natives David Hellman and Dale Beran, both 25, are childhood friends who deploy a seemingly organic style drawn entirely using a computer in the quest for whatever makes them laugh. "I used to be a middle school science teacher, but I quit," says Beran. "A Lesson Is Learned..." won the 2005 Web Comics Choice Awards for Best Layout.

TED RALL: How did you two meet and decide to collaborate on "A Lesson Is Learned"?

DALE BERAN: We met at a bowling alley. No, wait, we met at school, at the Park School, in Brooklandville, Maryland, near Baltimore, in ninth grade. Which was a long time ago, I guess. We weren't very good friends at first. We were into slightly different things but our spheres of adolescent interest sort of met.

And those interests were...?

DAVID HELLMAN: I think Dale found me obnoxious at first. I didn't mean that was one of Dale's interests, though it may have been. Sometimes I believe he is actively working to undermine me.

DALE: I think we just didn't jive because we each doing our own self-involved thing in a very boyish way. But yeah, our interests were somewhat close so we talked. I read comics and sometimes drew them. David was into anime and video games and I liked those things.

DAVID: In ninth grade, Dale belonged to a pack of intellectuals who looked like vagabonds and passed around Neil Gaiman and Frank Miller comics.

DALE: That's true.

We looked homeless. Most of the school was carpeted so we spent a lot of time on the floor with laptops, naively debating philosophy.

What made you decide to collaborate on a webcomic?

DALE: By the end of high school we had become friends, then bitter enemies, then friends again, then there was college in which we both floated in a strange haze. Then after that we decided to make webcomics.

DAVID: You're skipping over the tragic crush we both had for the same girl, which drove us violently apart and then brought us back together in the end, which I feel we should begin promoting as part of our mythology.

We collaborated on projects over the years, including

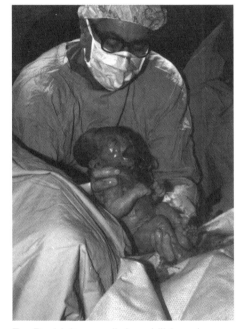

For David, it was all downhill from here.

a feature-length film my younger brother made when he was graduating from high school. His friend who was writing the script was crazy, so he asked us to do it.

DALE: Together we wrote a two hour screenplay.

DAVID: I like to think of it as our "Apocalypse Now." You have no idea the hardship of making this movie. Actors defected and their absences had to be written into the story.

DALE: The movie was filmed with me as the lead. It's not so bad, but very strange.

DAVID: I appeared briefly, looking uncomfortable as I recall.

DALE: He was the assistant to the villain in the boardroom. Did you have sideburns then?

DAVID: I had a wolfish unkempt look.

DALE: For awhile, we had both dropped out of college and lived together free in a renovated barn on our friend's large property. We called this place the Flophouse.

"Another day," thought Bear, "of mind-shattering executions."

DAVID: I was collecting cheap N64 games. I would go to Target and bring back large plastic balls that would bounce crazily, that we had no room for.

DALE: I beat Turok Dinosaur Hunter. I was working at a comic book store. Eventually we both went back to college.

DAVID: I don't think that's true. I remember you were playing Turok 3 but you got frustrated and quit.

DALE: Dammit, I think you're right, that's so like me. The webcomic started after I graduated from college and came to Baltimore, I think.

DAVID: Basically, the collaboration came out of that male way of hanging out and making each other laugh combined with our independent impulses to make things.

DALE: We also had a regular jogging schedule.

How did you develop the deadpan tone and subject matter of the strip?

DAVID: It's deadpan? I thought it was frenetic and unhinged. But I'm not arguing with you. Actually I find that interesting.

DALE: It maybe takes a thin line sometimes, which could be considered deadpan. The humor isn't evident. It has to be eked out in a sort of abstract way. You have to walk it around a corner.

DAVID: I would never call the comic's tone "understated" but I guess we don't put the funny bits in italics or anything.

DALE: But David is right, most of the humor and the character of the comic comes from just what we find funny between the two of us and maybe a close group of really funny friends.

The plots are unhinged, certainly, but the dialogue invariably starts out deadpan. Then everything goes haywire.

DAVID: Right.
DALE: That's true.

Like the one about murdering the Shaolin monks, where the killer comes home and digs straight away into his roommate's pizza.

DAVID: Dale's scripts often begin with a proclamation of some kind, like "I've become a master of kung fu!" and then some bizarre events spin out from there.

DALE: Another critic said that we mixed the banal with the insane or something like that. I think it was the banal and the surreal, which is true.

DALE: The comic started off very down-to-earth. It was supposed to be about us. Then the rocket ship launched out of control.

DAVID: Well, Dale can speak for his writing but my perspective on it is that he likes forcing dissonant things into a weird harmony. It's very free-associative. Often I get a script and am rather perplexed at how it came to be.

DALE: Inevitably it's that life is very strange, cruel and unpredictable, which I like to emphasize.

DAVID: But I think collaboration is excellent this way because it forces one to enlarge his sensibility.

DALE: Between the two of us we find a funny synthesis of sense and nonsense, I'm usually the nonsense half.

DAVID: And I'm incredibly serious. All the time.

What's your division of labor? Who does what, in what order?

DAVID: It starts with hanging out a lot and talking about whatever, which is kind of like spreading mulch around.

DALE: He often stabs my smoldering cigar butts with his umbrella tip and looks exasperated. He loves it, in fact.

DAVID: Dale, are you going to help me with this gardening metaphor or what?

DALE: Soon, the locusts arrive.

DAVID: Seven years famine.

DALE: Uncle dies in a plowing accident. The children starve. I am sent into town to trade my magic beans for a cow. Or the other way around.

DAVID: Well, from this shared context, Dale goes off and writes something. He'll show up at my place and we'll read through the new batch of scripts.

DALE: I usually write several scripts at a time, and David chooses the ones he likes.

DAVID: I usually get them in the order he's written them, so the first one might be a little stiff and disjointed but the next one will be more relaxed. It's interesting to read that way. Sometimes it takes two stories for Dale to really hit the nail on the head or sometimes it's the last one that really works.

DALE: Then we work through what we want to do with them, what he likes, what I

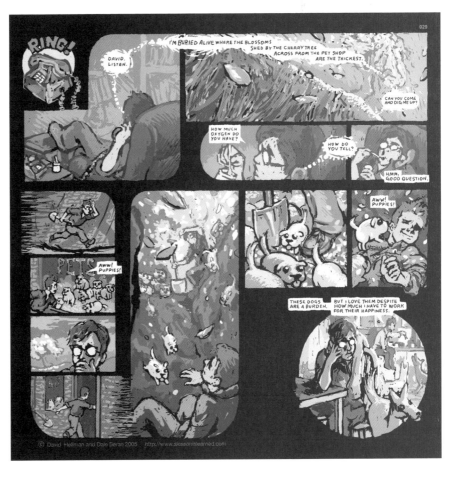

DALE: When I met David in ninth grade I was impressed with him as an artist. He was better than a lot of the artists in comics I read. He seemed to work the opposite way I drew. When I drew it was very messy and I would eventually sharpen things up. But he is a very neat artist, and things come out very clean. Now he likes to make things messy. A lot of comic artists strive to be "super-clean."

DAVID: Art school helped me think about the entire picture, rather than putting things into a picture.

DALE: That's what's popular these days.

DAVID: I like objects to look inextricable from their surroundings.

The effect is striking, different from other strips, organic and dark.

DAVID: Thanks, I like the word organic because it suggests everything is part of one. Also, I'm drawn to work that looks like the result of a struggle.

DALE: If you haven't noticed, we like struggling.

DAVID: As though the whole thing somehow found its way through the atmosphere, twisting and burning, to arrive before me. And that gets to the subject matter of the comics as well.

DALE: It goes well with the "there are many problems arising" theme of the scripts.

DAVID: That's partially our sense of life being full of madness, ups and downs, of many things being arbitrary, but at the same time very stimulating.

DALE: Things look inextricable and the problems are inextricable.

Does the collaboration ever risk harming your friendship?

DALE: No. I think we could harm our relationship, comic or not. If anything, we are both happier when we are making things and being productive, so in general it's a soothing thing for both of us.

DAVID: That's true.

DALE: Just having an audience who like we do is really good for us.

No one watched our movies but ourselves. We thought they were hilarious.

DAVID: Dale has been in Brooklyn while I'm still in Baltimore, so not jogging together and that sort of thing has

---

like, what should change.

The fourth script is easier than the first one and usually much different. There's a secret archive of never-used scripts.

DAVID: Then I think about the whole thing and try to come up with a way to frame the events of Dale's story.

DALE: David is always displeased with what he does and goes through a million drafts and I am pleased with pretty much anything he shows me. But usually, as he works on the comic, we talk through what he is doing.

But for the most part I have this absolute freedom at the beginning portion and can do whatever I like—knowing that at some point it will have to encounter David in his role as editor—and then David has a different sort of freedom in interpretation of what I give him.

So, David, you do the drawing. Where does your drawing style come from?

DAVID: I don't know where my style comes from. I get uncomfortable when anyone asks me about influences, but I've been drawing with a Wacom tablet [a device via which impressions made using a stylus appear on a computer screen] and naturally the qualities of that medium exert an influence over my style. Most of the episodes are drawn with a one hundred percent opaque pencil or brush tool in Photoshop and I erase as much as I draw—or draw one color over another, as the case may be. My lines are not very elegant, but I constantly carve back into them. Some people have said the comics look like woodblock prints and that's why, because the way I draw is like carving. I like the mess that results.

made the collaboration more difficult. So I guess I answered your question backwards. The collaboration really depends on the friendship.

DALE: That's true.

DAVID: So in a Machiavellian sense, I really value Dale as a friend.

David, are you planning to follow Dale to Brooklyn?

DAVID: I'm thinking about it.

Because of the strip?

DAVID: Yes, but not just that. I've been feeling like getting away from my hometown, and New York City is obviously full of itself and many interesting things. But as I near graduation and the reality of leaving begins to solidify, in a way I've gotten cold feet and I'm just not sure what I'm going to do.

In the meantime, do you exchange ideas via e-mail, phone, or both?

DALE: The whole deal. I still go down to Baltimore sometimes. David has come up once or twice, as well.

DAVID: Yes, and e-mail and the phone fills in between.

Is it helpful in any way, or is the long-distance friendship more of a stop-gap measure?

DAVID: It's much better when we're near each other. I can't really think of any advantage to being apart from each other.

DALE: Yeah, the ideas are flowing.

DAVID: Although I've had much more time to be alone.

DALE: Which we both enjoy.

I was thinking that you might be more focused on the work when you talk.

DALE: I think that actually hurts.

DAVID: Really?

DALE: When we talk and its all about the comic, it doesn't allow time for the mind to relax.

DAVID: I don't need to relax. I need to be more tense.

DALE: If we're talking once or twice a

week, it's only about the comic. It doesn't leave room to joke around.

DAVID: Oh, I understand,

DALE: I mean most of the time when we hang out we don't talk about the comic. We play music, or trash-talk our friends or something.

DAVID: I'd interpreted the original question as meaning "when we talk—when we're nearby each other."

But you meant, now that we're apart, when we work it might be better. It's sort of a drag to always have to talk business.

There's always something that needs to be dealt with.

Do you guys hope to make a living as cartoonists?

DALE: (laughter) It would be nice to live off any creative endeavor.

DAVID: Yes. It might not always be comics, but I want to be able to work on my own projects. The money question is looming larger and larger.

DALE: That's the idea for me, too. I'd like

to make a living off my writing in some way. Whether that's novels or comics or poems. It makes little difference to me.

DAVID: So, either "A Lesson Is Learned" will have to become much more lucrative, or hopefully it will lead into something else.

Have you had any interesting money-making possibilities crop up?

DAVID: I'm personally very encouraged by the reaction to this comic. It shows that if you make something of a reasonable level of quality with something interesting about it, the Internet will respond. Women shove dollar bills into our belts all the time—but seriously, nothing we can talk about yet, but several people have contacted us.

DALE: That's what was so wonderful about the Internet. It was a way to connect immediately with an audience, without an editor. And it worked well for us. As for money making possibilities, we're selling posters because people kept wanting to buy something. And most of the time that was posters and as David put it, that's the "most honest" thing to sell rather than coming up with a bunch of merchandise.

DAVID: Although we're not against that sort of thing.

DALE: C'est vrai. We're ready to sell out at the drop of a hat.

In fact, I have my suitcases packed.

Dale's early attempts to woo the ladies.

Ben Smith

Political commentary that revels in the artistic and editorial freedom of the Web

In addition to his Web site, Ben Smith's "Fighting Words" appears in *Flak Magazine*, Comics Sherpa, Webcomics.com and OnlineComics.com. He also enjoys a following among the denizens of the left-wing blogosphere's high-traffic sites such as Buzzflash, Jesus' General, Pandagon and Cursor. A native of Seattle, Smith is currently, as they say, "between day jobs."

TED RALL: Why did you start "Fighting Words"?

BEN SMITH: Probably because I felt compelled to produce some kind of commentary given the way things were/are going in our country. I was working in a large law firm, trying to decide if I wanted to go back to law school, but I was probably going to get fired eventually because I was spending most of my time on the Internet reading current events, etc. Also, since it was New Orleans, I was among a select few in that office who held the political views of the liberal persuasion, so I tended to be a little antagonistic about that with some of the other people working there. Otherwise, I absolutely loved living in New Orleans.

Why a comic strip rather than, say, a blog or column?

I've been drawing comics since I can remember, but I had put it aside for about ten years (since about the time I finished high school). So it occurred to me, while I was contemplating what career path I wanted to take that I had a skill there that was just lying dormant. Also, having gone through the readmissions process for law school several times, it occurred to me that one reason I had problems there was because of the low value law school places on passion and creativity.

I realized that I had a certain drive to create, that wouldn't

necessarily be satisfied by the legal profession. Also, I just couldn't wrap my brain around the idea that your arguments don't emanate from your own moral framework but rather from a set of rules laid out by statutes and case law. I do enjoy the writing aspect of what I do—which is probably obvious, and I just started up a blog, but the cartoon format just feels right for the type of commentary I'm trying to do.

You peripherally referenced the verbosity in your cartoons. I've found over the years that some readers refuse to take the time to read wordier pieces because they're "too much work." Do you get that reaction? Does it concern you?

I get that reaction a lot and I do take it into account, but I've got to be true to myself also. Probably the most important part of commentary for me is the process of coming up with a solid argument. I don't think

FIGHTING WORDS
by Ben Smith

IN THE FUTURE, AMERICA'S FAVORITE REALITY TV SHOW WILL BE REFORMATTED!

Fear factor 2048

...WITH ALL NEW STUNTS THAT REFLECT THE CHANGING TIMES, INCLUDING:

EATING A FRESH-CAUGHT FISH!

Ewww... WHAT'S THAT SILVER STUFF OOZING OUT OF IT?

MERCURY.

BARF!!

GOING OUTSIDE WITHOUT AN OXYGEN TANK!

COUGH COUGH COUGH COUGH HACK HACK!!

30 MORE SECONDS!! YOU CAN DO IT!!

WALKING ON A BEACH!

KEEP GOING DUDE!! ONLY 20 MORE FEET!!

OOOOOH!! HE GOT ANOTHER SYRINGE IN THE FOOT!

TOXIC KEEP OUT

DRINKING A GLASS OF TAP WATER!

JUST CHUG IT, MAN!! JUST CHUG IT!!

(WHIMPER) I... CAN'T... DO... IT...

© 2005 Ben Smith

that can really be accomplished with just a drawing and a few words which inevitably will just be a comment on some surface aspect of the larger issue at hand. I tend to rail against anti-intellectualism in our political discourse and to do the classic editorial style cartoon would in my case probably be a little hypocritical. I choose to believe that my audience is not going to be scared off by having to read a bit.

"Fighting Words" is primarily distributed online. Is this by choice, or have you submitted to print newspapers and magazines?

Print publication is definitely a part of my plan. I've mostly been online because that's where it's easiest to be seen, especially starting off. There aren't a whole lot of money-making opportunities on the Web, though, so I think print is still where it's at. From what I've read, the Internet is the future for our business, especially given the fact that the profession of classic editorial cartooning seems to be shrinking fast.

Yes, but what's the profit model? How do cartoonists of the future—people like you—make enough money to quit their day jobs?

Well, I'll let you know about future success when it happens. Right now, I don't know if most of us can quit our day jobs. Personally, I rely on part-time jobs and a lot of support from my family. Plus, in my years I have become a bona fide expert on putting together meals for less than three dollars.

FIGHTING WORDS
by Ben Smith

1991

YOU THINK THIS IS A **REAL** WAR? YOU'LL NEVER HAVE TO EXPERIENCE THE HORRORS OF WAR LIKE **MY** GENERATION DID IN THE 60'S. I'M TALKIN' **SCORES** OF FLAG-DRAPED COFFINS, **UNSPEAKABLE** ATROCITIES COMMITTED AGAINST PEOPLE IN THEIR **OWN COUNTRY**, VIOLATIONS OF INTERNATIONAL LAW, UNCHECKED CORPORATE WAR-PROFITEERING, AND THE **UNENDING FUTILITY** OF A WAR WITH NO CLEAR MISSION AND NO EXIT STRATEGY...

PERSIAN GULF WAR

1994

YEAH, THAT'S TRAGIC, BUT NOTHING LIKE THE LEVELS WE SAW DURING **VIETNAM**. ASIDE FROM ALL THE VISIBLE CASUALTIES LIKE KIA'S AND AMPUTEES, THERE WERE UNTOLD NUMBERS OF "**INVISIBLE**" INJURIES LIKE POST-TRAUMATIC STRESS DISORDER, WHICH RESULTED IN WIDESPREAD HOMELESSNESS AND ADDICTION AMONG VETERANS. AND A LOT OF THEM WERE WORKING-CLASS KIDS JUST LIKE YOU WHO GOT **DRAFTED**...

GULF WAR SYNDROME

1999

YOU CALL THAT A **PROTEST**? BACK IN THE '60'S WE KNEW HOW TO STAGE A **REAL** PROTEST... IT WAS A CULTURE WAR THE LIKES OF WHICH THIS COUNTRY HAD NEVER **SEEN**! FAMILIES WERE **TORN APART**! AN ENTIRE GENERATION WAS FORCED TO GATHER TOGETHER TO SPEAK **TRUTH** TO **POWER**! THANK GOODNESS YOU WILL NEVER HAVE TO EXPERIENCE SUCH TURBULENT TIMES...

SEATTLE WTO RIOTS

2005

YIKES... GOOD LUCK, KID...

MANDATE!

© 2004 Ben Smith

My favorite for a while was going to the corner gas station where I could get a can of chicken noodle soup, Sierra Mist and a bag of Doritos for about a dollar-seventy five. Voilà, one meal.

Funny thing is, once you start running in major publications, everyone thinks you've made it. Which you have. But you're not rich. When my mom's friends saw my work in *Time*, they asked her when I was going to buy her a new house like Mike Tyson did for his mother. There isn't a pot of cash at the end of the rainbow—in this business, making the rent from your art is success—but people still want to try it anyway.

I think a lot of people see certain folks like Ruben Bolling ["Tom the Dancing Bug," *Attitude*] and Aaron McGruder ["Boondocks," *Attitude 2*] get movie or TV deals and cling to the possibility of riches beyond our wildest dreams. I probably do too, but I just want enough to live and pay off my student loans!

But even that stuff is a chimera. I don't know about those two deals but most cartoonists get "development deals" where they have to work like dogs for maybe a few thousand bucks over many, many months. It's surprising how little money there is, even when you "make it."

But enough whining. What's with Fuzzy Bunny and Honey Bear?

You mean, are they a little too "friendly"? Who knows? That's

their business, I suppose. I came up with that concept after reading a great six-part series by a Seattle-area writer named David Neiwert called "The Rise of Pseudo Fascism." It occurs to me that many of us live in a sort of children's television-like "Happy-Land" where that sort of thing couldn't really happen. I tend to think that our democracy is more fragile than that and requires a lot of care and attention to keep it together. I went to see Bill Moyers speak not too long ago and he said he thinks the last time democratic politics failed to the level they are currently was during the civil war.

There's tension when cutesy animal characters discuss deadly serious topics like war and corruption. And it's funny. But does it trivialize the issues at hand?

I don't think so, if the issues are discussed in a serious manner. I think what it's satirizing is the reaction of these cutesy little characters when they're confronted with issues of such magnitude.

To play devil's advocate from both sides in fewer than fifty words, perhaps more humor would help your message go down more easily?

Yes, you're right, and I think that's the trick to great satire. It is something I haven't mastered completely yet, but I'm endeavoring to become much better. Take some of the old episodes of "The Simpsons," like the one where Mr. Burns runs for

Smith and his mother in Yakima, Washington, after Mount St. Helens erupted in 1980.

governor. Those are really great, in that they're making a comment on something but within the context of the story and these characters. So, I guess, the commentary isn't really explicit, but still powerful and entertaining. Another one of my influences in terms of popular writing is the early seasons of "The West Wing," the episodes written by Aaron Sorkin. I think the commentary is more explicit there, but the writing is just so graceful and smart that it works. That is really something I aspire to do.

Your work has grown by leaps and bounds artistically and in a very short time. You've gone from black and white to full color, from single to multiple panels, from stiff typeset word balloons to elegant, natural-looking lettering. What happened? Are you indulging in a highly illegal drug that other artists should know about?

Just dedication, my friend. And a call from my student loan officer from time to time doesn't hurt my motivation. I will say that Photoshop is an incredible tool. I would urge anybody who is serious about cartooning to learn as much about it as possible. Every day, it seems like I'm coming across some little trick that makes my work better or makes the job easier.

If you could choose between the following, which would you choose: (a) become a full-time cartoonist? (b) US withdrawal from Iraq, but you spend the rest of your life working at a shitty job you hate so much you can hardly believe it?

Wow, tough question. I suppose the completely altruistic answer would be (b), but I don't think that would be honest. I truly believe, as Moyers said in his speech that our form of government needs argument to survive. Given that, in the grand scheme, Iraq could just be the start of many bad things to come with the current leadership, having more people willing to speak out is probably a good thing. The part about me not ever having to sit in a cubicle again is cool too, though.

You're a tough cookie.

M.e. Cohen

Traditional editorial cartoonist resorts to the Internet

At 46, M.e. Cohen is a virtual senior citizen in the virtual world of Webcomics. A humorous illustrator who has published nearly 10,000 illustrations, "HumorInk" is an editorial cartoon that appears regularly on numerous Web sites. His cartoons have appeared in *Time* magazine, the *Los Angeles Times, Asbury Park Press* and about 100 other publications. His previous projects include *National Lampoon's* "He" and *Newsday's* "Bottom Dollar."

TED RALL: You fit pretty neatly into the genre of standard daily newspaper editorial cartooning. Have you looked for a job at a paper?

M.e. COHEN: From your lips to G-d's ears. [Editor's Note: Some people believe that writing the Name risks erasing or defacing it.] I have looked for jobs at the dailies. The usual suspects from the past couple of years: *The Buffalo News, The St. Louis Post Dispatch, The [New Orleans] Times-Picayune.* As you well know, that pretty well sums up the job openings from the past year or two. Maybe if I wasn't an atheist, G-d would have given me one of those gigs.

Don't forget the *St. Petersburg Times.* That's the latest one.

It's interesting that you say that I "fit nicely into that genre." First off, I take that as a compliment. I've always tried to be subversive in a daily sort of way. The main complaint from dailies about my work is "You're too harsh." I do walk a fine line. I try and mix it up. I've heard that I'm hard

M.e. Cohen & sons

to peg and I believe that is difficult for editors.

So what did the (rejecting) editors say about your work?

I have to paraphrase based on my recollection. "Too harsh." "Too one-sided." "Write funnier jokes." You get the gist.

It's not not a compliment. I've always wanted a job at a daily too—though I'm beginning to wonder whether I'll ever land one. Have your applications to the dailies been ignored or have you received specific feedback from editors?

Both. I've received standard rejections, specific feedback, and have been ignored. I don't take well to being ignored. If a paper

PROMISE ME THAT IF THEY TIGHTEN THE BORDERS YOU'LL FIND A WAY TO CONTINUE CLEANING MY POOL.

M.e. CohenHumorInk.com 03.23

asks for submissions I believe they have the responsibility to at least get back to you. If it's a form letter I understand, due to the sheer volume of supposed submissions. When I'm ignored, I usually push back with a phone call, e-mail, letter or something.

I agree, a rejection letter is courteous. But I hardly ever see one these days. So is your Internet presence more of

an outlet in lieu of a spot at a daily paper or a continuing online portfolio, or what?

It's absolutely "The outlet." I came back to political cartooning for very specific and different reasons than most. As you know, I am not a young pup. I've been in the illustration business for many years now, making a nice living and raising a family. Although I love the illustration

biz, it can be a bit disposable. One day it's okay and the next you're lying on the floor of the subway. No real impact or legacy.

After September 11th everything changed for me. New York City was my home for twenty years, some of which were spent just a few blocks from the World Trade Center. After that day I looked at my two sons and wanted them to know that I was contributing in some way. The most logical thing for me to do was to return to political cartooning.

What kind of feedback do you get from your online readers?

They run the gamut. I have a few groupies that trade my work back and forth. Some people seem to get what I'm trying to do. Of course the most enjoyable feedback is from the "haters." At first it kind of freaked me out but then I learned to embrace it. I work in a really small universe across a big globe—readers from all over the world. It's interesting because I don't think that their numbers are all that large.

My career as an illustrator has always been based on large numbers of people, mass publications. This thing is much more personal. There really is no ulterior motive here, just one guy who gets to say, draw and write whatever he wants. Not large amounts or money involved, not a large ego. I'm through with that. For me it's like this ongoing performance art piece, the first real art that I've been involved with. The numbers of people do seem to be growing and I do like it when they get it.

Has the site generated much paying, print work?

It's minimal compared to what I've established over the years. In fact, I may be paranoid but it might actually sometimes work against the more commercial work. What normal-thinking right-wing editor wants to work with a crazed leftie, no matter how funny or clever my illustration work might be?

So you basically do it because you have to, because you're driven by your artistic and political muse?

I know that sounds pretentious and self-righteous, but yes. My days have become about two hours longer, waking around 5 a.m. just to fit it in. Although I will say that once you start it becomes like an addiction. It's hard to give up the junk, of hitting the nail on the head.

Did you feel the same way under, say, the Clinton Administration?

No. I was living in my own selfish, deluded world. Very focused on getting it all together for my family. I'm the first to admit that I was/am a Clinton supporter, even though he broke my heart.

So what are the issues that really get your juices flowing?

Allow me to quote myself: "Angry is no way to go through life. Unless you're a political cartoonist." I usually start from that space, what is making me angry today. Hypocrisy, hubris, arrogance, irresponsibility.

For a long time I couldn't decide if I hated George Bush or not. At first I even felt sorry for him. Then I said to myself, screw that, I hate this guy. I hate this guy because he knows that he's not smart enough to be the leader of the free world, yet he took the job anyway.

A much younger — and much inebriated — M.e. Cohen in college.

Bread and butter: one of the Cohen's magazine and newspaper illustrations.

Who are your artistic influences?

George Grosz [German Expressionist Painter, 1893-1959], Johnny Carson, pre-pedophile Woody Allen and Francis Ford Coppola.

Wayne Stayskal [editorial cartoonist for *The Tampa Tribune*]?

I'm afraid not. It's funny; there aren't that many cartoonists that I'm into. Never was big into comics, although I did love *Mad* magazine and *Playboy* (for the cartoons also) when I was growing up. There are a couple of guys working today that I admire, but for the most part I just can't take it.

Evil question time, then: Who are your least favorite cartoonists?

I'm not wimping out but, offhand, I can't think of any names. There are so many guys at dailies doing the exact same cartoon everyday that they all meld together. Drawing style means little to nothing to me. It's the concepts that make me want to fall asleep. Sometimes mine included.

How would you distribute your cartoons without the Internet?

I wouldn't. If it weren't for the Internet I would not have the heart to do what I do everyday.

Why Wayne Stayskal? Does my work remind you of his?

Yes.

Argh.

I think he's a good, loose artist.

I like his drawing style as well. It's just that half the time, like most guys today, I don't know what he's talking about.

Politically?

Politically we're just opposites. That's fine. I truly love the left/right dialogue. It's just that I don't get the concept most of the time. Maybe it's my fault. I faintly remember enjoying his work much more a few years back. Maybe it's his recent stuff that has fallen off for me.

What advice would you give a young cartoonist starting out today?

Buy oil futures.

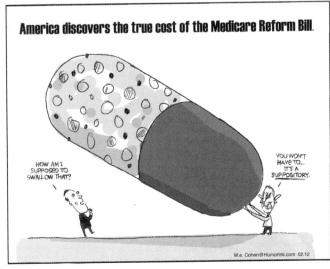

Dorothy Gambrell

Arch, wicked and cruel – like life itself

"Cat and Girl" revels in a brand of archness perfectly suited to the frequently tone-deaf Internet. A native of Long Island, New York, the 27-year-old Gambrell supplements her income with CAG merchandise including the ingenious "Donation Derby": you pay her money and she draws you what she spent it on.

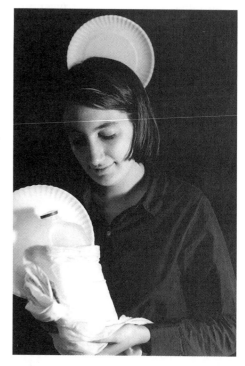

TED RALL: First question: I'd be remiss were I not to ask you whether you have a cat.

DOROTHY GAMBRELL: I live with my gentleman friend and he owns a cat. But "Cat and Girl" predates both cat and gentleman friend.

So "cat" isn't your cat. Is "girl" you?

Both of the characters are me in the way that any character has to carry bits of its creator with it to be true. No character is me more than any other.

That's unusual. Most cartoonists use one character as an alter ego. Other characters are usually foils and/or based on other people they know or have met.

I don't recognize a very clear line dividing "based on people you know" and "based on parts of yourself." If the habits or affectations or deep personality quirks of someone are the ones you would select to create a character from, I think there must be some kind of recognition in yourself. I mean, unless it's Lorenzo the doorman or "South Park"'s Timmy or something.

"Cat and Girl" takes on seemingly random subject matter. Do you see the strip as a way to express whatever you feel like at the time or are there topics you like to come back to?

I like having the freedom to draw a cartoon about whatever I've been thinking about recently. There are some things that I find myself thinking about again and again, to the point where the world does not demand another "Cat and Girl" cartoon about the empty facades of ironic T-shirts or America's invisible class structure.

Although fans want to see every successful joke repeated ad nauseum.

I sometimes make jokes dependent on cultural references that maybe twelve people will get. And readers indulge me. They don't mind not getting a joke immediately if it means that they spend a discrete half an hour at work trying to find out why Tom's of Finland baking soda toothpaste is

The Numbers Racket

IQ.

ERA.

MUSIC CHARTS, MOVIE REVIEWS AND ZAGAT.

VIEWING THE WORLD, BUT ONLY SEEING THE RANKINGS AND NUMBERS.

HOW MANY STARS DO I GET FOR WAKING UP THIS MORNING? IS THIS A TWO THUMBS UP MOUNTAIN?

FOREVER QUANTIFYING.

HOW LAME IS THAT?

EIGHT.

funny. Ending every comic for a month with a repetition on a theme can work very well. But since I am lucky enough to have readers who don't mind working for the punchline, I would feel like a cheater if I didn't work for the punchline in every cartoon too.

However, as you know, many readers aren't willing to do any work while reading a cartoon. Do you care?

My goal with "Cat and Girl" was to draw the cartoons I wanted to draw and not censor anything because it's too obscure. There is a point where obscurity is an obnoxious ploy to place yourself above others, but there's also a point where removing anything obscure becomes talking down to people. Not talking down to people has somehow got "Cat and Girl" from taped-up flyers in a miniscule Massachusetts town to more people than I've ever met reading it every week. There are people who don't want

to do any work and there are plenty of people who find my cartoons painfully pretentious and forced and incompre-

hensible. There are lots of other cartoons they would probably enjoy more. I find "Penny Arcade" incomprehensible. I'm

Dorothy Gambrell

not willing to work to understand it. I think they're doing okay without me.

Nostalgia, i.e., the "good old days," is a recurring theme in "Cat and Girl." Why?

Nostalgia lies. People might have been able to leave their doors unlocked but they also ate their vegetables out of cans, and most rural families didn't have electricity or indoor plumbing, and medical treatment was often clueless if you were lucky enough to afford it, and people worked until they died, and, oh heck, there were some pretty awful race and gender predicaments—it might be easier to just carry some keys around.

But nostalgia is so powerful that even knowing the lies it rests upon doesn't stop it. I'm suckered into it all the time. Remember four years ago, when Chengwin wasn't so crowded and Ray still worked at Great Lakes? Wasn't that great? Remember three years ago when we had the larger apartment and we could be loud late at night and have big parties? Sure, there was no heat in the winter and in the summer the garbage trucks parked outside the window and we all had the worst mosquito bites of

our lives. And then we got kicked out for being loud late at night. But wasn't it great?

You've mercilessly lampooned ironic/hipster T-shirts. Do you ever wear them?

I have a T-shirt that bears the name of a camp I have never attended. It cost a dollar at the Unclaimed Baggage Center in Scottsboro, Alabama, and I desperately needed shirts. I am slightly ashamed of it.

Early "Cat and Girl" features typeset word balloons. Why did you switch to hand lettering?

It's actually the typeface "Kid Kosmic" from blambot.com. I switched to a more cartoony typeface because an overlong spiel about being and nothingness looks more inviting that way. There's more tension between a polished cartoon bubble and

half-formed rants about the patriarchy than there is when the rant is in a typeface that is already halfway to term paper.

"Cat and Girl" has quite a following online. Have you been able to translate your audience into an income?

Cat and Girl Order Out

Does the money come in through reader donations, or what?

Most of my income is from selling "Cat and Girl" T-shirts and oddities from the Web site. There's another decent chunk that comes in from "Donation Derby" and occasional money from cartoons and odd jobs and medical experiments.

So you sell hip T-shirts too?

Oh, they're not very hip.

Your sardonic tone can be jarring, as in your strip "Morning in America." "Shuttle Disaster, Seven Dead" is a lead-in to a droll punchline: "The '80s are totally back!" Do these cartoons get you into trouble?

I received a concerned e-mail after "Cat versus Hobos," in which I extended indie culture's fetishization of failure to the Democratic Party. I was told that the

I have reached the point where I can make a living from drawing cartoons. This living does not include luxuries like drying my clothes at the laundromat, but it is a living.

Mysteries of the Unknown

Panel 1: ...UFOS, ATLANTIS, THE LOCH NESS MOSTER.

Panel 2: I MEAN, IF ATLANTIS IS REAL THEN WHERE IS IT? / BERLIN.

Panel 3: HUH? / BERLIN.

Panel 4: WILLIAMSBURG BEFORE THAT.

Panel 5: THE LOWER EAST SIDE, THE LEFT BANK, ZURICH — IT MOVES AROUND.

Panel 6: BERLIN ISN'T THE DOMAIN OF POSEIDON! / THAT PART'S JUST A RUMOR.

Panel 7: YOU'RE TELLING ME THERE'S A SECRET HIPSTER SHANGRI-LA...

Panel 8: THAT MOVES AROUND AND IS CALLED ATLANTIS. / YEP.

Panel 9: CAN I COME? / UH –

Panel 10: WHY NOT? / I'M COOL!

Panel 11: RIGHT?

Democratic Party was doing a great many positive things on the local level and my pessimism was not helping.

Is this type of reaction why you don't do a lot of politics?

Not at all. I don't mind reactions. I enjoy thinking about culture and society, our class and economy-based social hierarchies, how culture-identified subgroups suspend and uphold different class markers, the loud soup we all live in and how it's navigated and how it's self-policing. This just interests me more than confronting politics directly does, though I can recognize politics as a definite motivating force behind these issues. And there are already plenty of interested people dealing directly with politics.

Last question: Does being a female cartoonist on the Web draw unwanted attention from male fans?

I haven't had that experience. I do try to keep a certain distance between my personal life and my life as it is lived online, but that has nothing to do with gender. I'm just a quiet person.

Thomas K. Dye

What if "Doonesbury" only ran online?

"**N**ewshounds" uses a traditional comics trope—talking animals—to comment on politics and current events. Thomas K. Dye, a 36-year-old Las Vegan, previously published a strip called "Pet Sounds" for the *Berkeley Voice* and the *Montclarion*. His day job is as a secretary at an insurance company.

TED RALL: What do you hope readers get out of "Newshounds"?

THOMAS K. DYE: Mostly, I hope people are able to look at an issue and see that it's relatively complex and yet interesting enough to explore. When you have a host of talking animal characters, there's a hope that the very oddball dynamic involved will bring a twist to whatever sense of normality we're currently living these days. Moreover, because you can make any human being you want be barefacedly greedy, deceitful, and two-faced, you can expose that hidden nature of humanity and present darker motives plainly. But dark or light, issues are still so multihued that you still are allowed to think about them, even if you're laughing at the same time.

"Newshounds" runs in the traditional horizontal daily comics format and, like "Doonesbury," it's a continuity strip—you have to follow it every day to understand the jokes. Was that your original goal, or is it currently your desire to get picked up by a syndicate and distributed to daily newspapers?

I'm really not interested in newspaper syndication for "Newshounds" anymore. That was my goal at the beginning, but it became obvious to me that newspaper editors are more interested in strips that can be cut out and push-pinned to the office bulletin board. I had always hoped that I could fill the niche of "Bloom County" or "Doonesbury" but I don't see that niche as available anymore. People are a lot less likely to follow something regularly in a newspaper the way they used to.

The only recourse for a continuous-arc comic became the Internet. As for the horizontal daily comics format, I've stuck to it largely because it represents a form of discipline. With larger, page-sized cartoons there's a tendency to sprawl and develop a leaden pace. With the more

Dye at 19.

compact format, you get more said in a lot less time.

Since you're committed to being seen mainly on the Internet, have you considered altering your format to something that fits the screen a little better?

There have been times when I have toyed

with a fuller-sized comic or color, but I still see the traditional format as the most dynamic for my purposes. I also have a strong desire for book publication, and Plan 9 Publishing has helped that to become a reality as well. To me, there's something special about a comic strip collection that a graphic novel can't convey. There's more value to each page; there's more said in every panel; and there's a near-guarantee that you'll get a punchline or a climax at least every page. So if I do ever alter the format, it would be with similar publication ideas in mind as well.

You're a traditionalist! Most younger artists lust to put a successful graphic novel under their belts, sell the film rights and retire to Malibu to have sex with surgically-enhanced people.

Yes, but of course I'm not writing about genetically-enhanced Goth future warriors walking slowly towards you. Oops, did I say that? It does also help that I don't exactly trust Hollywood in general. I've always felt that if "Newshounds" were taken on by a major studio, eventually it would be rewritten to the point where Renata's gay co-worker helps her with dating advice. I like the format as it is because it allows you to quietly soak it all in and process it your way. Not the way that you're expected to take it.

Do you get a lot of feedback from your readers?

I get enough to help me see how certain things are being taken. Most of the character-driven narrative is the material that gets the most response, which is ironic, because when I began I was sure no one would be interested in my characters at all. At the beginning, my comics tended to force-feed character traits onto the reader. But when I found that character growth was a better conduit for

getting a point across, I just let things happen and the response has been very satisfying as a result.

You're a traditionalist in this sense as well. You have characters, not "characters" who serve as ciphers to deliver lines—something pioneered by "Life in Hell" during the 1980s. Is one of them your alter ego?

Kevin is who I really am and Alistair is who I'd like to be all the time. There's a bit of me in Ferris as well; his pop culture obsession represents a side of me that I don't care to cultivate, but it happens anyway. But Kevin is who I feel I really am; someone stuck in a whirlwind of activity that other people are always causing. In the meantime, I'm just sitting here, writing it down, processing it, trying barely to make sense of it. I've had people disappointed that he seems to be only a straight man, but there's more to a straight man than people think. If you didn't have the bulwark of Pogo or Charlie Brown, there would be no center to measure the crazier lunatics against.

My wife says the key to comics success is cute animal characters. Do you subscribe to this theory?

If I did, I'd probably be a lot more bitter than I already am. Actually, if you're going to have a successful cute animal in a comic, better it be a nonentity who pees in the corner than a central character with any depth. As for me, the animals represent an easier way to speak about human foibles. Sometimes I think it's bad enough being human, let alone having a host of human-wannabes trying to imitate all their transgressions. The latter idea makes it more interesting to me; dogs and cats in real life really do think we're the greatest species on earth because we provide food and shelter. When

Dye at 34, with "Alistair."

they gain language and deeper sentience, that translates into slavish imitation. Not that I believe an essential part of humanity is being an emotional Xerox of the guy next to you. No, not me.

You began "Newshounds" in 1997, during the height of the Internet boom. Did you ever land any lucrative offers back then?

Not at that time. I did have some success with some of the single-panel material I was doing before then, but that was marginal. It was only just before the bust that the offers came, and of course by then it was too late to really make anything from it. Internet business sense, for the most part, had been characterized by a throwing-mud-at-the-wall approach and I saw that even then. But since syndication was become increasingly out of the question, I took what I could. I was fortunate that under the circumstances my choices seemed to be well made. The offers I rejected quickly petered into nothing. And I thought I had no business sense at all.

Do you see a financial future — making a living from — "Newshounds"?

I think there's always hope. I feel there are a few marketing angles I

say than I know what to do with. I think even if I had "Newshounds" as a day job, I would still be putting in sixty-to-eighty-hour weeks, which would make me not so much fun at parties. Right now, the extras that I have to put in to the books to make them more marketable are a good way to get my excess artistic energy taken care of. The regular pace of the Internet comics serves that dual purpose. I get to express myself regularly with an audience and at the same time I develop some sort of credibility that draws people in.

At the beginning those deadlines were sometimes a burden, but there was hope I would become rich. Now I don't think I'll ever be rich, but deadlines are a breeze. You might call it a strange "professionalism high."

It's funny how people always ask how cartoonists come up with ideas. Ideas aren't a problem for good cartoonists.

If you're just looking around, ideas just happen.

What's your worst fear?

I don't know what I would have told you if you'd asked this a month ago. Now I read about melting Arctic ice sheets and bird flu viruses that the U.S. Health Department can't cope with, and I hope that even if I'm just living in some modest apartment in a college town, that in forty years there will still be a world with some beauty left in it. My threshold has sadly gone down some.

I just want to be able to have the freedom to continue doing what I'm doing. For that to happen, the world needs to be here. Let's not rush to prove the doomsayers right, hmm?

haven't tried yet. Since it all comes out of my pocket to advertise or promote, progress is always slow. But, in general, it may not be "Newshounds" that puts food on the table. I have a few other ideas that I'm going to try to put out there in the cartooning world, ideas that I feel have a saleable nature and yet don't fall into any cookie-cutter formats. But "Newshounds" will always be a part of

what I do. I have difficulty imagining not having these characters around in some fashion. They fit very comfortably into my world of expression.

So it's really about keeping yourself sharp as a cartoonist? Deadline pressure helps you focus?

Oh, absolutely. Because I have more to

Eric Millikin

Fulfilling the terrifying promise of the teenage notebook cartoon

"Fetus-X", drawn on notebook paper and deploying a drawing style that crosses Edvard Munch with an incipient victim of high school suicide, is the brainchild of Eric Millikin, a 32-year-old who once dissected cadavers in an anatomy lab. His comics and illustrations have run in the *Detroit News, Metro Times, Lansing State Journal* and serializer.net, earning him two Society for News Design Awards of Excellence. In 2000, the Catholic League claimed that "Fetus-X" "regularly ridiculed Jesus."

TED RALL: "That's not a real cartoon!" Do you get that reaction to your work?

ERIC MILLIKIN: Sure, I've gotten that reaction quite a few times—from editors, readers and even other artists. I've had readers write letters to editors explaining that "comics are supposed to be funny" and they don't think my comics are as funny as "Garfield" or "Judge Parker" or "Gil Thorpe." Editors are usually easier to deal with, because they sort of know what they're getting into before they start running my stuff, but occasionally an editor leaves and then I've got to try to explain myself to

them—comics are an art form, artists are supposed to experiment, if it wasn't dangerous it wouldn't be rock and roll, whatever. I've had new editors say things like "Maybe I'm not taking enough drugs, but I just don't understand this at all."

The reactions from other artists is probably the least important but the most puzzling. From them I get things like, "It's not a cartoon because it doesn't look like ninety-nine percent of all the other cartoons. I don't use that typical goofy cartoony style with super simplified and exaggerated figures, the stark black outlines, all that traditional stuff that's grounded in

part upon the really bad printing presses of the early 20th century. I also get the "That's not comics" from artists who read in a book somewhere that comics equals "sequential art" and therefore if you don't have at least two panels in a row you're not making comics, no matter whether it says "comics" at the top of the newspaper page right above my "not comics," or whether my pay checks say "comics" on them. And those are all interesting discussions sometimes—"What's a cartoon?" "What's a comic?"—but I'm not at all interested in changing what I do to satisfy somebody else's idea of what a comic or cartoon ought to be. I'm more likely to do the exact opposite. I'm interested in cartoons unlike any I've ever seen before, and if no one else will make them, I will.

If I'd seen the stuff I wanted to read in the paper, I wouldn't have become a cartoonist.

Exactly. I think my motivations are probably about ten percent the occasional "Wow, that's cool, I wish I'd done something like that," and ninety percent the "Wow, that's shit, I'm going to do better than that."

What's with the gothic/graphic atmosphere of "Fetus-X"—the killer kittens, the "Night of the Living Dead" para-noia? **Are you cartooning's Rob Zombie or are you trying to convey something deeper than an aesthetic sensibility you happen to find appealing?**

The gothic atmosphere is coming from a few different directions. First I've always been into horror movies and stories. I grew up in the late '80s, taking girls out on first dates to see slasher movies and everybody trading their Stephen King novels back and forth and even the music. It wasn't Rob Zombie at the time but I remember in Detroit Alice Cooper coming out of retirement when I was in the eighth grade was like the second coming of Christ. So a little bit of just whatever I do is going to be at least a little bit horrific.

But I think political horror comics are perfect for what's going on right now. Everything our government does is based on fear: "If you don't elect me, terrorists will kill you" or "Welfare moms (not Halliburton) are stealing all your money" or the classic "We can't wait for the smoking gun to come in the form of a mushroom cloud." We've even got a president who's so inarticulate that, because he can't handle a four-syllable word, had to declare "War on Terror" rather than "War on Terrorism." And I'm sitting here with a copy of Edgar Allan Poe's *Tales of Terror* that I've had since elementary school going, "We just declared War on What?"

And of course horror has always had an element of social and political commentary to it, whether it's *Frankenstein*'s fear of scientific progress or *Dracula*'s fear of sexuality or even just the general horror concept that "those that are different from us must be destroyed." That was what I always like about the '70s zombie movies like "Night of the Living Dead." They took the horror genre's typical conformist "the outsider must be destroyed" theme and turned it into the opposite, where it was instead the majority of people that were zombies and so we were cheering on the minority struggle.

I could go on and on. *The Communist Manifesto* starts out as a ghost story: "The spectre of communism is haunting Europe." And in comics, I can think of at least one artist who draws the president as a complete psycho with fangs. I'm sur-

prised more artists aren't making political horror comics. I'll happily accept the "Rob Zombie of cartooning" title.

Do you really draw your comics on lined notebook paper and tear it out?

Yes, I really draw my comics on lined notebook paper and tear it out, I really did find an Egyptian mummy sitting on my toilet, and George W. Bush really was the world's greatest alcoholic war hero in the Texas Air National Guard. The notebook paper, believe it or not, was the result of years of painstaking research and soul searching. I'm knocking down a barrier that I think comics throw up which is that really nobody makes comics—and here I'm talking about the "comics" of the "Hey, that's not comics!" vigilante justice squad. I think horror, like most other genres, is best when it's told in the first person. "This horrific event happened to me and I almost died" is generally more effective than "This horrific event happened to him."

In prose, in short stories and novels, the first person makes sense because you can actually believe that somebody would sit down and write paragraph after paragraph about the horrific chain of events they've fallen prey to. In the traditional comics format, that's just not believable. Nobody, after surviving a zombie attack, is going to sit down with a sheet of two-ply Bristol board and a blue pencil and a number two crow quill pen and start drawing by-the-book "sequential art." It's got to be more raw and more real. Like notebook paper, and handwriting, and dark expressionistic figures.

And if you think about comics as this anything-goes art form where you get to combine words with pictures in any damn way you please, then you start to look at things like Da Vinci's notebooks and say, "Hey, those are comics." And then I think, "if I were Lovecraft's Herbert West, Reanimator, what kind of comics would I draw?" They'd be like Da Vinci's, they'd be like lab notebooks, horrific diaries, they'd be sort of like mine.

Notebook paper also elicits the first medium used by most budding cartoonists—the stuff they have available during class.

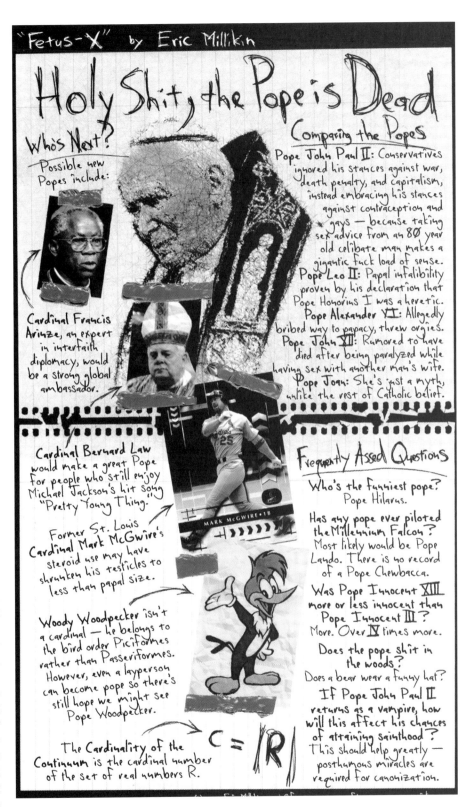

Oh, yeah, it's what we all started with. I remember drawing little comics in class in the fourth grade and selling them for a quarter. I remember when I was three years old drawing comics of whatever I wanted to dream about, then rolling them up and sticking them in my ears before I went to sleep.

I vividly remember having a nightmare while I was toilet training, I must have been younger than two, where I was standing up (like a big boy) and urinating in the toilet when a ghost came up next to me and started peeing in the toilet too. And then the toilet starting overflowing because I guess that ghost really had to pee. He must have drunk a lot of ghost beers or something. Anyway, of course I knew I would be blamed for it because nobody else believed in ghosts and so that was really scary. Combine the fear of ghosts with the fear of toilet training and punishment and so of course I woke up and just had to draw some pictures

about this. So, making horror comics has been my way of making sense of the world pretty much since I could pick up a crayon.

Horror comics on notebook paper. Horror comics on the backs of my grandmother's grocery receipts. In kindergarten I got busted for drawing pictures

of my teacher naked with no head (I can't remember what that was all about). In the second grade they would make us draw birthday cards for all the faculty members even though we were only seven years old and we had no clue who these people were. So my natural reaction to having to make a birthday card for one of the lunch ladies was to draw her a little comic where the candles on her cake burnt out of control and burned down the school and then I signed it "Fuck you." That one went over real well.

But, anyway, yeah, political statements with horror comics. The targets have changed a bit since I was in elementary school, but hopefully I can draw and express ideas a little better now.

Man, I gotta go back that school and see whether they really put those in my "permanent file."

What is the future of "Fetus-X"? What careerist ambitions, if any, do you have for your strip?

Right now I've got what seems like a fairly sizable online readership—which of course I'd like to grow—but those are all people that come back because they know they're going to like what's next and they'll agree with me on what I'm saying and write me these "Right on!" e-mails which are great but I feel like I'm preaching to the choir sometimes. Which don't get me wrong, that's got its place—there were years there when it seemed like so few people dared to question the President of the United States that it was

Millikin with his cat, Charlie Monster – a frequent model for his cartoons.

Dec. 9: It's been two months since Alicia and I boarded ourselves up inside this house to protect us from the demon kitten. How much longer can we last?

Dec. 10: My God, He's out there feeding on a child's arm. Or is he bringing it to us as some sort of a "gift?"

That arm looks vaguely familiar.

December 11: Perhaps I've seen that middle finger before?

Dec. 12: A child's lower leg.

Dec. 13: Today, a hand.

Dec. 14: A kid's ear.

Dec. 16: A leg bone.

If this keeps up that cat could destroy as many children's lives as the Catholic priest who helped form NAMBLA.

Dec. 17: the demon cat's latest "gift" looks like a butt cheek. It's big and hairy – I'd say it's not from a dead kid like the others were. It must be a more adult butt cheek. Hard to tell from this angle, but it could be my plumber's.

Weird.

Dec. 18: He's still out there, with the same butt cheek. Is he trying to tell me something?

Dec. 19: Again with the butt cheek. I feel like he's trying to communicate with me, as if that left butt cheek is a symbol. But what is he trying to say?

Dec. 20: For four days now that Satanic kitten has been out in my yard licking that bloody left butt cheek. The logic behind this evil still escapes me.

December 21: God help me I think the insanity makes sense to me now. That's not just some random body part; it's a chunk out of someone's ass. And not just any chunk, that's the left chunk. And that's an adult piece of ass, not a child's. Oh my God, is that what this is?

If it's not an adult's left butt cheek then it must be ...

No child's left behind?

When *The State News*, Michigan State University's newspaper, pulled one of Millikin's cartoons, at least they let readers know about it.

good for readers who hold unusual viewpoints to be able to read a comic and say "Yes! I'm not alone!" And I think you can take someone and push them to the next level, whether it's taking someone who's disgusted with our government and has never voted and switching their apathy into activism.

But there's part of me that wants to connect with readers that either aren't sure whether they agree with me, or even definitely know that I'm an evildoer who supports the terrorists and is hurting America — or whatever the title of the latest right-wing book is. I've got to reach that middle ground so that those people know that all the propaganda they see on the center-to-right, CNN-to-Fox news media doesn't represent at least a third of the country. And I think the people on the far right need to be reminded that no, they're not normal, and no, everyone else isn't like them. And I think the best place to do that is still in newspapers.

I know a lot of artists look at newspapers like it's a dying industry but it's still about the only place where you can put your comics in the face of someone who doesn't want to see them, or who isn't sure they want to see them. Somebody on the way to the sports page gets distracted by your comics and gets exposed to viewpoints that don't get expressed over at the water cooler or down at the yacht club or at the gym. I've had my comics in and out of newspapers, had the Catholic League calling the presidents of universities that run my comic in their student newspapers and by the time this book comes out I'll probably have been hired and fired from a few more, but that's actually where I want to be. I'm like Sisyphus, rolling a big crack rock of Fetus-X comics up a hill in Hell and I'm actually picking up steam on the way up. I'm in bigger newspapers then ever right now, I'm staying in newspapers longer, and I think it's only a matter of time before the Wall Street Journal starts running my comic on their front page.

So, yeah, anyone reading this book, pick up your local paper, call the editor, thank them if they're running good comics and tell them to run mine if they're not already. Just don't get anybody else in this book fired.

August J. Pollak

*Up-and-coming cartoonist/blogger finds himself
in the heart of the beast*

August J. Pollak, 25, is like many webcartoonists an active blogger, and he draws the "XQUZYPHYR & Overboard" comic strip for both his own Web site and CampusProgress.org. With a strong emphasis on politics and current events, Pollak's work is fueled by his current residency inside the Washington D.C. Beltway. He has self-published two collections of cartoons, *Ridiculously Simple Graphs and other Observations from XQUZYPHYR & Overboard* and *Monkeys Flinging Poo and Other Proud Moments in Media Punditry.*

TED RALL: Why did you name a character "XQUZYPHYR"?

AUGUST J. POLLAK: "XQUZYPHYR" is actually the first "handle" I ever used when I started using dial-up bulletin boards in the mid-'90s. I was in eighth grade at the time and just discovered all those little dial-up BBS systems. New Jersey was lousy with them at the time. This was right before the big AOL boom, right before the web started. I think the original gag was that since it was a username that was only online, I wanted it to be deliberately unpronounceable. It ended up continuing as AOL screennames, usernames on other boards, and eventually a comic character. When blogging started up and a lot of guys (Atrios, etc.) were using secret identities, it sort of fit the character retroactively. In their current form, "XQUZYPHYR" and

"Overboard" are sort of to me like the physical representation of anonymous webloggers and pundits who just sort of babble about whatever's on their mind at the time.

Much of your work is overtly political, not far removed from traditional editorial cartooning. Did you ever consider going that route?

Once. But to be honest, the biggest issue for me is the size restrictions. I start with the writing in my cartoons—the entire thing is scripted before I even start drawing. Very rarely do I come up with something that works as a one-panel gag. Some people can do both—Keith Knight, for example, does both a long-format strip and a single-panel, and they're both brilliant. I'm used to my strips almost being like something

that needs room for an introduction, a setup, and a punch line.

As for "traditional" editorial cartooning in general, I avoid that because my biggest fear when drawing a strip is that I'll do the same gag as someone else, and I think with the mainstream guys you get that way too much—like when a celebrity dies they all do the exact same thing. I have no desire to do another gag about Al Gore inventing the Internet or how Ted Kennedy likes to drink. I think most of my readers already know George Bush is an idiot. So I don't think that needs to be the gag. The gag should be about why he's an idiot. Or at least why he's an idiot this week.

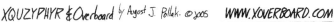

There's no physical space limitation online, but can readers be counted upon to read long-form comics?

There's this term in webcomics called "infinite canvas," which is the idea that with webcomics you can go far beyond print limitations—animations within panels, non-linear panel flow and so on. I'm not against that, but with my political strips I write them with the idea that people could read them both online and in a newspaper or magazine. I think readers don't have a problem with reading a long-form comic if they like it. In fact, if it's good, they should be happy it gives them even more than a typical newspaper daily. Matt Bors, Brian McFadden, Keith Knight, Ruben Bolling—I think the quantity of product they put into a weekly strip almost mandates that much space. It's tough because print editors want as small a space as possible to make room for another phone sex line ad—but to each cartoonist their respective canvas dimensions, you know?

Your characters look like they've been hit by a delivery van. Do you know a lot of accident victims?

I'm actually not quite sure what that means.

They're all scrunched up, with painful expressions.

A-ha. Well, much as I'd love to blame physical problems, I think that's just the way I draw. I'll admit there are irreversible remnants of my love for Garfield as a six-year-old. So I think the eyes sort of came from there. I've tried to make some elements a bit more detailed and others a little more streamlined. I was an animation major, so

one of the big lessons of drawing for animation is getting as much detail and definition of a character using as few lines as possible.

Like many webcartoonists, you couple your strip with a blog. Why do you feel the need to work in both media?

I started the blog because I only did one strip a week and wanted something to fill the site space between comics. My college roommate at the time, Chris, had started weblogging a year earlier and showed me the entire process and I realized it worked. Tom Tomorrow was really supportive of some of my early writing and directed a lot of people to the site early on, and amazingly some people are still around and think I write well.

I think the blogging has a great use for the readers though, in that they make you more familiar with them. I like the idea that people actually know August Pollak, not just "oh, I've seen that cartoon somewhere before." But if I had to choose, I'd rather be known as a cartoonist who blogs than a blogger who draws cartoons. I don't really think of blogging as a unique tool but rather a system that makes writing on a Web site easier. If Moveable Type vaporized into the ether tomorrow, I'd still write on my Web site.

What's your audience, i.e., what kind of people read your strip?

I don't think I have that many readers overall at this point, but of those that didn't merely find the site accidentally while searching for porn, I think it's a pretty good crew. I get a lot of blog links, but I also get links from

people mentioning the strip and saying "man, that's funny." That's the best feeling for me. I have readers that participate in random off-hand notions, too. I did a cartoon show a year or so back and, jokingly, I said I'll sign anything for readers, even their baby's head. So a

Ann Coulter

reader showed up with a plastic doll baby for me to sign. That's divinity, right there. I admire so many bloggers who use Web sites to promote progressive ideas and organize political action—I work in the same field—and I think that's what I enjoy about blogging. But I want the comics to entertain people above all else.

Do you think there's a certain demographic—men/women, under-thirty/over-thirty, cat owners, whatever—who gravitate towards webcomics?

I think there's a certain demographic that gravitates toward webcomic culture in general. Webcomics were dominated early on by the video game culture, which only until recently chose to market itself mainly toward young males with loads of disposable income. I don't think men dominate the web; in fact I think women have stronger voices in much of it—for example most web humor I read about pop culture is by women. But I can't think of that many female web cartoonists. I'm sure there are many and I feel like an asshole for not being aware

of them. By female web cartoonist I, of course, mean web-only. There are tons of cartoonists who are women whose work I read online: Mikhaela Reid ["Boiling Point," *Attitude 2*], Jen Sorensen ["Slowpoke," *Attitude*], Emily Flake ["Lulu Eightball," *Attitude 2*], and so on. I hate the myth that women aren't on the web, or that women don't read webcomics. I read tons of female bloggers, have tons of female readers and for that matter tons of older readers, gay readers, readers in the military, and so on. I think, and I hope, that everyone can do it. I have never read or not read a webcomic because of the age, race, or gender of the artist.

Cat owners are a completely different thing, however. Everyone with a blog has cats. It's like a rule. I have cats back home. I miss my cats.

What's your biggest regret as a cartoonist? As a human being?

I think my biggest regret as a cartoonist is that I didn't pay enough attention in the beginning to the best way to start out. I've been doing the editorial strips for six years now and I'm only just beginning to understand the actual process of trying to get my work out there. It probably connects to my human regret, which is my self-doubt and lack of initiative. I'm working on both of those and I think the response my work gets helps both of them. Recognition is without a doubt the biggest motivating factor in my life. It's nice to be appreciated; it's nice to be told you've done something. It's hard for me to actually accept that people like me and what I do. When I actually get confirmation of that, it feels like winning the lottery.

Mark Fiore

A survivor, Fiore is the only American political cartoonist to turn animation into a living

Mark Fiore has succeeded where internationally syndicated political cartooning icon Pat Oliphant has failed: he is the only full-time animated editorial cartoonist in the United States. The thirtysomething San Franciscan developed his Flash-based Webcartoons after a short stint at as the staff editorial cartoonist at the *San Jose Mercury News* turned sour. The first animated cartoonist to win the Robert F. Kennedy Journalism Award, he has also won an Online Journalism Award from the Online News Association and the Columbia Graduate School of Journalism. Because this book is inanimate, individual "cels" are presented in lieu of the real, moving, thing.

TED RALL: Describe your pre-animation career in cartooning.

MARK FIORE: Before I switched over to animation, I followed the fairly traditional path of selling print political cartoons to newspapers. After drawing cartoons for my high school and college papers, I began freelancing right out of college for a tiny free cartoon paper that paid nothing. Not peanuts—nothing. My first big break happened when I was living in San Diego for eight or nine months and came across a classified ad advertising a political cartooning job.

That is the first, and I'm sure last, time I'll ever see an ad like that. Anyhow, the pay was good, the weekly publications were targeted to military bases in the area and a few years into it, I realized the whole operation was a scam. Two years after these papers disappeared, I was visited by a Columbo-like inspector hot on the case of the mail fraud my former "editors" were committing. In short, my first well-paying freelance gig was a complete fraud.

I continued my freelance trek to Boulder, Colorado where I sold political cartoons to the *Boulder Daily Camera* and the *Boulder Weekly*, while initially supplementing my income by working in a porn mag distribution warehouse. While in Boulder, I heard that the *San Francisco Examiner's* cartoonist, Wiley Miller, had left his job as staff political cartoonist. I then began an intensive campaign to get a job with the *Examiner*.

This was before the Internet, so I subscribed to the *Examiner* by mail and it would arrive five days later. Then I would Fedex my packet of local San Francisco and national cartoons back to the *Examiner*, all on spec of course. I paid about a hundred bucks a month for the newspaper subscription, Fedex cost another twelve or so, and if a cartoon ran I made twenty-five dollars. Not a very smart business plan. It did, however, get me more in with a real-

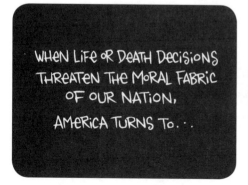

(What follows is a scene by scene breakdown of one of Fiore's online animations, complete with dialogue and sound effects.)

[Music: Cue disco music reminiscent of "Charlie's Angels" theme; song plays throughout entire cartoon]
[SFX: explosion]

Bush v/o: Good morning, Angels!

Angels: Good morning, Georgie!

live city paper. I met the last William Randolph Hearst, Jr. publisher, saw faxes pouring in from Hunter S. Thompson and generally became more fired up about a career in newspapers. Little did I know that this paper was on the way out and most other papers were soulless corporate black holes that sucked creativity from unsuspecting cartoonists' brains.

Long story somewhat shortened, I eventually moved back to San Francisco and continued to sell political cartoons to various (mainly California) papers. Then, around 1999, I started to experiment in animation using Flash. At the time, I still had to take the occasional non-political cartooning freelance job. This particular one involved creating Web sites and later a video to teach kids about Greek mythology. It was at that job that I began to see the potential for creating animated political cartoons.

I gradually picked up my first two animated political cartoon clients, the *San Francisco Chronicle's* web site, SFGate.com and MotherJones.com. Things were looking up, and then things really started to look up (or so I thought). Finally, I was offered a staff job doing traditional print political cartoons at the *San Jose Mercury News*! The brass ring I had been trying to reach since high school was finally mine. I took the job. It sucked. I quit/was fired and went running happily back to my freelance life and animation. After a little over a year of creating animation and traditional political cartoons for newsprint, I finally chucked the old style of cartoons in favor of devoting all my energy to animation. Since then, I've stuck to animated political cartoons.

Buster, the Friendly Nuke, is one of Fiore's reoccurring characters.

For you at least, animation has proven more stable and lucrative than static print-based political cartoons. But which do you like making better: print or Flash cartoons? If someone offered you a newspaper staff job doing old-school print cartoons, would you take it?

No, I don't think I'd go back to doing traditional print cartoons, even if they offered me a staff job with benefits and union heavies to break someone's knee-caps if I'd like. I still really love the old way of cartooning and do miss the single-panel format sometimes but the creativity and ability to get my message across is much more rewarding using

Fiore on the California coast.

animation. There are so many more tools at my disposal that allow me to get inside people's heads. Using motion, color, dialogue, sound effects and music

Bush: Well Angels, you've got lots to do today. You've gotta . . .

Bush v/o: ... Fight off a brain-damaged woman's husband!

[SFX: punching sound]

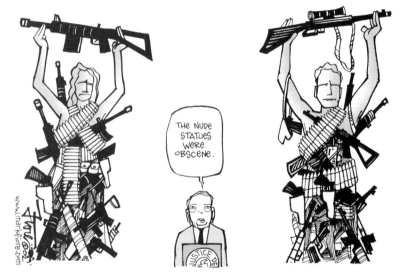

One of Fiore's print cartoons, before he left newspapers completely behind.

lets me do so much more than I could with a standard editorial cartoon box. I think I'd be frustrated if I had to go back to old-school print cartoons, I'd want to make people move and a music track play.

Is there a future for print editorial cartoons? You seem to have bet against it.

Yes, I think there is a future for print political cartoons. There will always be people that are compelled to create single-panel drawings that give an opinion. Of course, those are the cartoons that you may see tacked to a telephone pole, bashing the authorities, while the ones that are published in a major daily paper will point out the silly foibles of those gosh-darn Backstreet Boys. From a business perspective, I think the print political cartoon is on its way out. With most newspapers becoming more reluctant to take a stand and just trying to survive (or maximize their profits), why would they really be excited about paying someone whose job it is to bash people in power? That's why many cartoonists go the entertainment/gag cartoon route—that sells!

Is the market for Flash and other animated cartoons big enough to accommodate cartoonists looking to make the same move out of print that you did?

Yes, I think there is definitely room for others who want to make animated cartoons, Flash and otherwise. The tricky part is figuring out clever ways to make

[SFX: punching and kicking sounds]

Bush v/o: Force a feeding tube back into her!

Bush v/o: Choose life, dangit!
Choose life!
[SFX: glooping noises]

money, and that's where it helps to have at least a small entrepreneurial streak. I don't consider myself an entrepreneur, it seems more like "hustling." You've got to figure out a way to make some money doing what you love.

The days of falling into the traditional path of staff job and syndication are over, you've got to think on your feet and adapt. I've cobbled together a living by charging licensing fees to sites that want to run my animation and have more recently started to sell DVD collections of my work. Selling your work directly to viewers/readers is one of the great strengths of the Web and something that has a huge potential. Of course, first you've got to have an audience and then make stuff. (Stay tuned for Fiore Brand Malt Liquor.)

There is a market for people that are different. The web is a smaller world than print media. You can create cartoons for the *Podunk Weekly* and never worry about what the cartoonist for the *Bumblesticks Weekly* is doing. However, on the Web, since it's so easy to blip from one site to another, it's as if we're all in the same town, so originality has more value. A right-wing version of me would definitely be able to land some clients.

What kind of fits and starts did you suffer while becoming proficient at Flash?

As I mentioned, I was fortunate enough to learn Flash on the job while freelancing to support my political cartooning habit. I was in a room with two other

Bush as bumbling Agent 86. While Fiore draws on a small stable of friends for voiceovers, he does most of the speaking parts himself, including Bush.

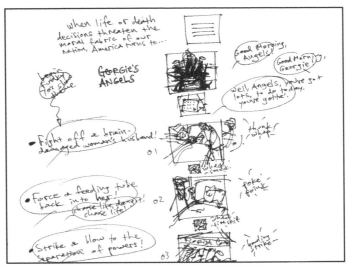

Before drawing and animating his cartoons in Flash, Fiore works out the details of each week's episode via storyboard.

[SFX: more punching and kicking sounds]

Bush v/o: Strike a blow to the separation of powers!

[SFX: pins being knocked over by a bowling ball]

As Republican scandals mounted in 2005, Fiore did "GOPS" – a take-off on Fox's "COPS, complete with bystanders' faces pixeled out.

Dude. Fiore is an avid surfer, and often spends mornings on the beach before heading into his studio.

guys and we were all learning at the same time. It was a great way to do it because one person would figure something out and shout out how to do X, and we'd all immediately be at the same level. Three heads were better than one. The first animated political cartoons I created took forever, what took me over a week then could now be cranked out in a day or less. The main hurdles initially were all time-related. Everything seemed to take so long initially, but that improved as I learned how to simplify. Having a good, concise storyboard in the initial stages saves an amazing amount of time down the road.

What do you think of your early work? Your stuff gets more sophisticated all the time.

My earliest work was basically just repurposed print cartoons. One of the first ones I ever turned into an animation was a multi-panel anti-gun manufacturer cartoon. I added eye blinks and the word balloons wrote on over the character. When I showed that to some people and editors, they were blown away. Golly, it moves! It really doesn't take long for people's expectations to rise (including mine).

First, just motion was enough, then a bit of sound, then dialogue, then more music, then fully orchestral music track, then custom songs, I've added all in varying degrees over the past few years. One thing I am careful about is adding new bells and whistles just for the sake of having new bells and whistles. Everything should still come down to

[SFX: even more punching and kicking sounds]

Bush v/o: Support the culture of life ...

[SFX: thunking noises as bodies fall]
Bush v/o: ... without bringing up the 152 people I executed when I was governor, mind you.

the idea and what conveys the opinion in the best possible way. The main reason that that early gun cartoon didn't have music or dialogue was because my skills and the bandwidth weren't up to it yet. I imagine I'll keep trying to raise the bar until my animation is more like an old Warner Brothers cartoon—which will probably require getting real animators involved.

Is your big goal a feature film?

That would be great, but I don't think so. I think short animations are more suited to political material, TV seems to be a better fit, although I'm sure that's a very long shot. "The Daily Show" [on Comedy Central] gives me hope for the future of satire. At some point, I'd also love to work on something that wasn't political but that feeling quickly passes once I get pissed off again.

Bush—as "Stay-The-Course-Man!"—lands on his face in Mongolia.

[SFX: more punching and kicking sounds, plus a screeching car-crash sound]

Bush v/o: And see to it that everybody lives the moral, upstanding life we tell them to live!

[SFX: popping sounds as signs appear; ventilator sound effect]

Bush: Well Angels, you've done another great job!

Bush v/o: God is real happy with you ... He told me so himself .... He said this is a great political issue! ...

[Bush continues talking as cartoon fades out] ... Whoops! In fact, I gotta' go, he's on the other line! ... Bye-bye, Angels.

Mark Poutenis

A veteran cartoonist puts his labor of love online

Perhaps because it's so obviously the product of a professional artist whose work appears in such publications as the *Phoenix New Times, Riverfront Times, Miami New Times, Cleveland Scene, Houston Press, NY Press, Boston's Weekly Dig* and *Sports Illustrated for Kids*, it's surprising to learn that "Thinking Ape Blues" is a more of a labor of love than a profit center for its 35-year-old creator, Bostonian Mark Poutenis. The reader feedback he receives from his online readers, along with those of the *Dig* and the *New York Waste* underground newspaper, keep him behind the drawing board.

TED RALL: Please describe the origins of "Thinking Ape Blues." How did you arrive at its current format?

MARK POUTENIS: Oh, Sweet Jesus, I'm already at a loss for words. No one has ever bothered to ask me about the strip, so I never thought I'd have to have an answer for this type of question. The only person who genuinely was "into" the strip was my old friend from New York, Iwona Awlasewicz, the Queen of Poland, but she was crazy and would laugh at "Last Tango In Paris."

At the risk of sounding like a pompous asshole, the concept of "The Thinking Ape Blues" dates back to the mid-'90s when I was living in New York City. I was in a weird power trio band called All-American Alien

Boy (named, by default, for an Ian Hunter album that neither of the other two guys had ever heard of) and I was the singer and bassist and songwriter (again, by default) and I wrote a song called the "Thinking Ape Blues." It was based around this bleak and nihilistic armchair philosophy concept about human nature and man's capacity to shit in his own nest, something other animals didn't seem to have, in my observation. Man sucks. He evolved into this cunning predator who turned to his intellect and craftiness to compensate for his shortcomings of being basically soft, clawless pink meat for bigger animals to eat. So, as he made tools and shelter and language and science and progress, he dominated the globe and finished first in the race. So what does this asshole do? He fucks the

whole thing up, trips at the finish line.

My favorite movie of all time, the one movie I would request to see if I had to die tomorrow, is [Stanley] Kubrick's "2001." And, like anyone who likes that film, my interpretation is probably different than the next schmuck. But for me, the lineage

THE THINKING APE BLUES by Mark Poutenis

STARRING THE **PROGRESS BROS.**

ABE

BEN

CARL

OK, these are Zener cards, used by some parapsychologists to test psychic ability. I shuffle the cards and hold them up, one at a time, so you can't see the face. You try to guess the sequence. With five different card types and 25 cards in a deck, you have a 20% chance of a correct hit. Anything significantly higher than a 20% success rate is supposed to indicate psychic ability.

Oh, this is such moldy horse shit and goat balls and you know it.

My hairy, pimply ass it is. I got fifty bucks that says I can do it, douche.

OK, so when do I double down?

Dude, you should probably just give me your money and I'll go buy you a 40 and some porn.

Aw, fuck you, man. I watch this shit on TV all the time. I got a system.

of ape to man to the next possible step, artificial intelligence (HAL, basically) was such a wonderful and romantic thing to ponder. Man was trapped between his base, primal self, his raw emotions and instinct, and the cold, mechanical logic of a machine.

So, man was the "Thinking Ape" for lack of a better term (I was in my early twenties and usually drunk and penniless, so this sounded like deep shit back then). And his "Blues" was the cold realization that as advanced as he was, as far as his species progressed, he was still just a dumb animal with a propensity to fuck up a good thing when he got it. The way he shits on our environment, both physical and psychological, the way he just savages his fellow man, the way he fails his friends and family, the way he hurts the ones he loves and says the wrong thing to the woman he loves and destroys his good thing. Of course, I'm married now, so I'd like to think my outlook has changed a bit.

So, anyway, the song was pretty bleak and angry. A few years later, I started getting work more and more as a freelance illustrator, and wanted to try my hand at a weekly strip for alternative papers. I was doing crap for the *New York Press* back then and was an enormous fan of Tony Millionaire's "Maakies." I guess he was the final influence to make me abandon any last traces of youthful desire to do "normal" comics and give in to the shit I always was drawn to, like the "Zippy" stuff and David Lynch weirdness; even though our art and writing is nothing alike, Millionaire, God bless his twisted drunken soul, was a real inspiration.

So I kinda drank on it one week at my drawing table at the Tower Records art loft, and was listening to my favorite Roger Waters album, "Amused To Death," and his almost gleefully nihilistic outlook for mankind really struck a chord with me. The idea of alien anthropologists finding the charred-out husk of mankind, their bones rotting in front of their TVs, well, that really jelled the thing for me. Of course, the Thinking Ape Blues! It wasn't an angry alt-rock song for a mediocre power trio, it was actually the blueprint for a comic where mankind

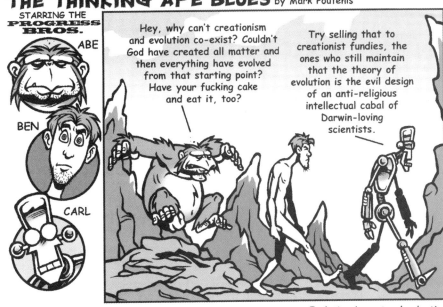

THE THINKING APE BLUES by Mark Poutenis

was the punchline and fuck it if no one else got it, it made me chuckle. I think, anyways, some days I'm not too sure.

Where do your central characters, specifically Ben and Carl, fit into this vision?

Well, the cheap, easy answer is that Ben is me but that's kind of a lie. I have a bigger beer gut than Ben and I wear glasses a lot now when I work. From your question, though, it seems you have a misunderstanding about the structure of the strip, which is kind of how I intended it: Abe, the oldest Progress Brother, isn't the Ape in Thinking Ape Blues. Ben, the

human, is. Humans are the thinking ape. Ben is that horrible, horrible, all-too-human anchor in that storm-savaged harbor of animal instinct and clear skies of logic and reason. To rip off a line from that '80s British comic "Miracle Man," "trapped between the heavens and the earth, the angels and the apes." But all three brothers constitute the Id, the Ego and the Super Ego of one psyche—mine, I guess. Hell, why not, right? I write this drunken gibberish, after all. They are the Moe, Larry and Curly of the psyche.

When we spoke on the phone, you mentioned that the strip isn't exactly a cash cow. Why do you do it?

Abe and Mark at the Association of Alternative Newsweeklies convention several years ago. Poutenis constructed the ape out of sculpted foam rubber and craft fur, over a PVC skeleton and random stuffing.

THE THINKING APE BLUES by Mark Poutenis

STARRING THE **PROGRESS BROS.**

ABE

BEN

CARL

So, to what do we owe *this* gathering of stereotypes?

Not *stereotypes*, asswipe, these are real, honest people with feelings and emotions who are tired of getting ripped on. These are our Amish brothers, our friends in the legal profession and our silent compadres in mirth-making.

These hard working lawyers, mimes and Pennsylvanian country folk are proposing legislation to prohibit the cheap comic crutch of using them for uninspired played-out hackneyed punchlines in crappy sitcoms and movies. When Hollywood, comics and writers make weak-assed jokes at their expense, they are insulting us all.

I see. And so you're more angry at the pathetic and unimaginitive humor than any real injustice.

Bingo.

And you wanna protect all stereotypes? Even rednecks?

Well, *of course* not rednecks. I mean, those toothless hillbilly motherfuckers are Goddamn hysterical.

More like a cash stillborn calf. I dunno. I work primarily as a freelance illustrator, so I get to draw for a living. It beats a real job. Sometimes it's tough, but I pull my half of the load most months. The thing about the strip is, and this will sound wildly high fallutin', it's basically a calling. I was going to pull the plug a year or two back when I was feeling the pressure of fatherhood (I'm a stay-at-home dad to a three-year-old boy) and deadlines and the feast-or-famine nature of freelance and I thought, "Fuck it, I don't need this hassle every Monday, wasting four hours on a strip five people may or may not read." I figured it was time for Abe to head to the mountains, Ben to suit up as the loneliest astronaut and Carl to start a ranch on Mars, but I chickened out.

Just as it was next to impossible to get this labor of love of the ground, it would be harder to stop it. I've been doing it for around five years. Why not continue? It has no rules, no storyline, just stream-of-consciousness bullshit that amuses me. Let's face it, since I moved back to the country in Massachusetts, I don't have many friends and I didn't have a lot to begin with in New York. What the hell else am I gonna do? I don't get a lot of feedback, but the feedback I do get is insane. It's crazy. I swear to God, I get e-mails from MIT professors, a guy at a research institute, a math professor, a guy who was into a ton of theological disciplines in some university—just weird, passionate people

I guess I'm like the NHL: most of the free world hates it or worse, is completely indifferent to hockey, but the loyal die-hards are insane and breathe that shit. If I get one e-mail a week from someone who gets it, and as long as at least my hometown longtime paper, the *Boston Weekly Dig*, keeps printing it, I guess I'll keep doing it, because it means I'm not alone in being crazy.

I remember an interview once with the guys who did "Mystery Science Theater 3000." One guy (the guy who played Crow in later years, I think) said that ninety percent of the people didn't get certain jokes that they would have in each episode, another five percent got it and didn't think it was funny, but for that other five percent, it was like that joke was written for them. They got it and it

THE THINKING APE BLUES by Mark Poutenis

STARRING THE
PROGRESS BROS.

ABE

BEN

CARL

Man, oh man, it's getting real ugly around here these days. People are dying at a ridiculous clip . . . and it all started, as usual, with alot of sanctimonious ass-wipes speaking on your behalf.

They say you want *this*, and those *others* say you want *that*, you love *these* folks more than those *other* folks, "You're on *our* side", "No you're on *our* side", this, that and the other thing . . . damn. It's like trying to keep up with *All My Children* while on a mescaline bender.

Of course, I just stay out of it all together, you realize, because I don't even believe in you.

Aw Hell, I don't even believe in me these days.

Poutenis multitasking. The stay-at-home dad makes his living primarily as a free-lance illustrator.

THE THINKING APE BLUES by Mark Poutenis

STARRING THE **PROGRESS BROS.**

ABE

BEN

CARL

This is Tina McGee. She was the girl who broke your heart in high school. Oh, sure, you never dated her, or anyone else for that matter, but you longed for her in the second row of Algebra. From her pink frosted lipstick to her pegged acid-wash Jordaches, everything about her made you crazy and inspired you to behave in a manner we refer to today as stalking.

Ocean Pacific

This is Tina McGee today, a spunky soccer mom of three. She might have a few miles on the tires, but still, alot of that girl-next-door is in her smile, and she can still make men commit strange, depraved and bizarre acts of self-loathing and deviation.

But to you, in your mind, Tina McGee is still that 17 year old heartbreaker with a glimmer in her eyes, a wiggle in her step and *Blondie's Greatest Hits* in her Walkman.

Christ, has life passed you by.

Would you leave me the fuck alone??

was a grand slam that would keep them chuckling on the bus to work for three weeks straight. That's the guy they fought to get that joke in for. That's the guy I waste my Monday nights drawing this crap for. I get one e-mail saying "Dude, that is so fucking funny" and they write me a three-thousand-word e-mail about it, that's why I do it.

Although a mass audience would be nice.

Well, of course. I'd sell my fucking soul in a minute if it meant I could feed my son and wife and impending daughter, but it ain't gonna happen. I'd be happy if I could pay the utilities with this stuff. But, basically, I was scared to stop the strip. I did a strip after year two that had the guys in front of a firing squad, blindfolds on, no one saying a thing. Then Carl and Ben sniff, and Ben says to Abe, "Did you cut one?" and Abe says, "It was the dog." After a pause, both Carl and Ben say simultaneously, "Dick". I was gonna end it on that, but I just had to see what happened next.

If the Internet hadn't come along, would you still be drawing "Blues"?

I think so, because of the loyalty of *The Weekly Dig*. They print it, so about sixty thousand drunks on barstools in Boston can use it for a coaster each week and I have no idea how many people see it on the Web. I don't even have a counter on my Web site. I'm scared to find out I had four hits in the last month, you know? At one point, I was in six alt-weeklies, and it really felt like I was getting somewhere with it, then typical media consolidation, every paper has to run what the *Village Voice* or the *New York Press* or the *LA Weekly* is running, I got dumped by a four-paper chain and a small paper in South Carolina in one depressing week. That was it, death to the Progress Brothers. I was gonna off them and get on with my life. But I hadn't made up my mind how I was gonna do it by deadline for *The Weekly Dig*, so I did another strip. Then my wife just said why not still do it? If it made me laugh and someone would still print it, why not?

It beats joining a KISS cover band at

THE THINKING APE BLUES by Mark Poutenis

STARRING THE **PROGRESS BROS.**

ABE

BEN

CARL

Huh ... What do you know? It's the End of the World.

Really. Hmm. How odd.

That really is something, huh? Who'd of thunk it?

I didn't think it would be like this. I always assumed it would be with a bang, a build up to a point in time, a zenith, a denouement, then ... poof. Not a physical place like a Shel Silverstein cartoon.

Yeah, I mean, you're walking through life, then whammo- it's the End of the World. I guess that's that then. Over we go.

Not necessarily. If it's a physical point, who says we have to cross it like lemmings? Who says we can't just turn back?

©2004 MARK POUTENIS

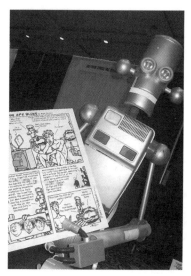

Carl (left) as a "big ass promotional prop" for Poutenis' booth at the AAN convention. Carl is made of PVC pipes, plumbing pieces and junk Poutenis found on the street. Iggy Pop (right), an illustration for the DIY 'zine "Creamy Fist."

thirty-five years old or paying a therapist to listen to me. And the Internet is a bizarre animal and webcomics are a pathetic animal. There are millions and most really, really suck. I mean, you may hate the "Thinking Ape Blues," but you'd have to admit, even if the art isn't your cup of tea and the jokes make you want to punch the family cat in the groin, it appears to be made by a professional. About ninety percent of these webcomics are either drawn by amateurs, kids who jack off to too much anime, or oh too-cool übernerds who think a cut-and-paste strip designed in Illustrator on a Wacom tablet with a punchline about how lame you are if you don't have the latest video game platform—it's no wonder I have no presence out there.

I'm a too-old and too-dumb animal to figure out how to market myself in the print medium, so how the hell am I gonna figure out how to make a blip on the radar on the Internet? I mean, I like my Web site, and it helps me get some readers in places like Iowa or Colorado, but I have no idea if anyone really knows a thing about me via the Internet. I guess I should learn, but I've always been my own worst salesman. I just wanted to do a comic that made me laugh, and it doesn't seem to fit into any of the accepted templates, and not in some groovy hipster outsider way, in a sucky way. I avoided political stuff because there was so much of that already and I was doing political stuff for the *New York Press* at the time, anyway. And I don't do slacker jokes like all those self-indulgent webcomics (although, as my brother-in-law, who's a professor at WPI and likes the strip, pointed out, the "Thinking Ape Blues" is the zenith of self-indulgence—an inane comic crafted for an audience of one.)

I just thought, was it so wrong to just wanna do a funny comic for a change? I mean, it may fail at that goal a lot, quite miserably, but it tries to be just something that might make you laugh over a beer once a week, using the tried and true ingredients of most of Western Culture humor: drinking, pointless violence, bullshit Reader's Digest philosophy, apes, robots, nihilism and the occasional appearance by Cheap Trick or Grand Funk Railroad. Why not? Indeed.

THE THINKING APE BLUES by Mark Poutenis

STARRING THE **PROGRESS BROS.**

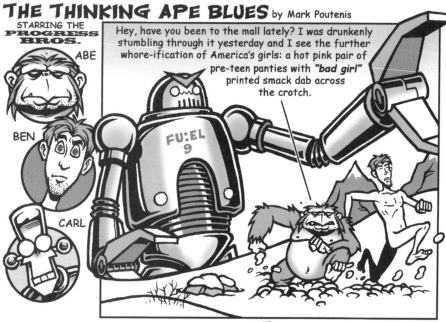

WWW.THINKINGAPEBLUES.COM

—END—

Nicholas Gurewitch

Pain in suffering, wrapped in soft gauze and fluffy pillows

Nicholas Gurewitch's "Perry Bible Fellowship" is a webcomics phenom, having leapt from widespread popularity among the technorati to such mainstream print media outlets as the *UK Guardian, Maxim* magazine (UK edition), *NY Press, Boston's Weekly Dig, Portland Mercury* and *Baltimore City Paper*. Gurewitch's twisted blending of the cute and profane, which sometimes recalls Neil Swaab's "Rehabilitating Mr. Wiggles," won the Web Cartoonist Choice Awards for Best Short Form Comic and Best Comedic Comic and the 2004 Ignatz Award for Best Online Comic. Gurewitch, 23, is also available to babysit.

TED RALL: Your artistic influences seem more opaque than most of the cartoonists who appear in this book. What are they?

NICHOLAS GUREWITCH: Frank Frazetta [fantasy and science fiction artist known for his paintings of Conan the Barbarian and Tarzan, 1928-], as I'm sure most people would agree, is a master at capturing movement and emotion. Though I am humbled every time I look at his stuff, I constantly aspire to make my frames communicate as effectively as his paintings. His characters provide anyone who looks at them with an impeccable idea of what is happening, and more importantly, what will happen in another given second.

Where does the surreality come from?

There's something special about taking an idea that occurs in reality, and taking it elsewhere. An idea is often made very clear to me if I bring it into a world that doesn't even exist. Or maybe I just like weird stuff. I don't know.

A lot of your humor involves violence, but the horror is tempered with a gentle, sweet tone.

A lot of gentle, sweet people are capable of doing things that could be described as violent. I suppose I've taken notice of this.

You see guys dynamiting pigs?

I've seen guys grossly miscalculate outcomes at the expense of someone else, yes. People with good intent often "dyna-

mite pigs"—proverbially speaking.

So does your strip often function as an allegory or, in the spirit of its name, a parable?

I think it's easy to see how most of them can function allegorically. I'd say most funny stories resemble parables because

Nicholas Gurewitch

truth is a common element in each.

Where does the strip's name come from?

It's actually borrowed from something written on a poster that my friend Albert found. I'm not fond of inside jokes, but I suppose it is a great big ol' inside joke that means a lot to me. I also really like the words in it, and how absurd it is as a name for a comic strip.

A lot of altie strips are named that way. And I'm pretty sure "Calvin & Hobbes" comes from the first line of a famous treatise on American history.

I think Watterson had better reasons than most people.

What's the best reaction you've ever gotten to a cartoon? The worst?

This guy once e-mailed me to say that one of the primary reasons he married his wife was because they could laugh at a certain PBF comic strip together. Apparently for long periods of time. The worst reaction was probably from this kid who said he had dreams where he was one of the characters from the comics. He claimed to have a very deep emotional connection with him. It's very interesting, but apparently it was an obsession that was getting him in trouble at school. I worry that he is looking into things too much.

It's never good to become the center of a reader's obsession.

And then talk about him insensitively in an interview.

Especially in a nation with easy access to firearms. Why don't you use more words? Is that a limitation you placed upon yourself?

I simply find that the quicker a comic can be read and understood, the narrower the margin of disappointment. It also excites me to think that foreign people could read some of the comics, and still be able to get something from them.

So how do you feel about wordy cartoons? Are any of them good because they're wordy?

Yeah, certain brave comic-creators take the risk, and succeed. "Bob the Angry Flower" [by Steve Notley, "Attitude 2"] and "Daily Dinosaur Comics" [by Ryan North, page 115] come to mind.

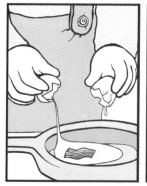

A still image from a 2003 PBF movie adaptation "A Kiss for Joe."

Robert T. Balder

A pioneer of political clip art

Robert T. Balder, 37, is a full-time data analyst who draws—or cuts and pastes—the online editorial cartoon "PartiallyClips" for such venues as the *Anchorage Press, Cleveland Free Times, Concord Mirror, East Bay Express, Houston Press, Manchester Mirror, Metroland, Nth Degree, Salem Observer* and the *Other Paper* as well as nthdegree.com, get-nifty.com and richfantasylives.com.

TED RALL: I'm sure people have pointed out the similarities between "Partially Clips" and David Rees' "Get Your War On." Who was first? Were you inspired by his work?

ROBERT T. BALDER: Ah, yes I do get that one a lot, and "Red Meat," [by Max Cannon, *Attitude 2*] too.

I was first, having been publishing in the format I use now in 1998 for Scene magazine (now defunct). David had his comic online before I did. But it was about eight months into the official "Partially Clips"-named project that I ran across GWYO. I can't claim much of an influence from GYWO though I admire the strip and find it hysterically funny most of the time. "Red Meat," on the other hand, both preceded and influenced "Partially Clips." But I have tried (maybe even too hard) to differentiate what I do from what Max Cannon does.

There's an evolution in your work. Did you ever consider giving up the clip art approach when GYWO became such a phenomenon?

Oh quite the opposite. GYWO's success gave me a great deal of encouragement. I think you might have inadvertently hit on the rift between two paradigms. For the most part, webcomics creators don't look on other comics as the competition except maybe in some abstract way. Print comics generally play a zero-sum game, in that there is finite real estate in target

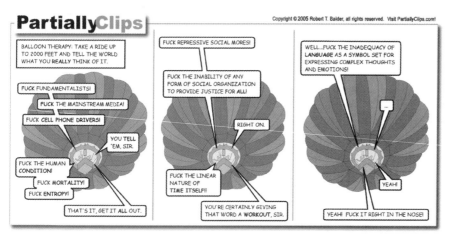

papers and he whose strip occupies the most real estate is generally the most successful.

Webcomics is a non-zero-sum game, in which it's still possible for the addition of a new and good comic to expand the total readership for all webcomics, a net benefit to the system and possibly to all creators. I think webcomics folks tend to be a lot chummier for that reason, more supportive of each other's successes.

But there's still trash-talking. Surely you must be accused of "ripping off" Rees.

The trash-talking in webcomics is largely confined to a few people who like to scrap, and a few hot-button issues on which we all tangle from time to time. I really haven't had much of a problem, either with being accused of ripping off Rees, or with people who openly followed my lead. There are comics out there who credit "Partially Clips" as an inspiration and who follow a similar clip art format. One guy I know has a decent strip that not only uses the same clip art in three panels, it's usually the same art from strip to strip. It's at http://www. angriestricecooker.com. He's openly blogged about my strip's influence on him, and I'm just fine with that. There's an evolution going on with webcomics themselves, and I'm happy that "Partially Clips" has had a role in that. It's far from done evolving, though.

Have you talked to Rees?

No, I've managed to talk to close to everyone whose work I have admired in webcomics, but both he and Max

Geeks R Us: Balder gets a Dungeons & Dragons calendar for Christmas (left). Every page was pinned to his bedroom wall for years to come. Old skool console gaming on the Atari 2600 (right) with best friends Geordie and CJ, dressed as the Three Musketeers on Halloween night.

Cannon I have never had the opportunity to meet. It's a shame. I'd like to ask him about giving away his book revenue and a few other things I'm curious about. I just mean, if I understand what he did, it's kind of indicative of why we're blighted with "Garfield" and not any good and challenging writing on the comics pages. Mercenary minds versus sincere artists.

If you need help giving away book or any other kind of revenues, I can take it off your hands. What gets you up in the morning, what motivates you to do each day's strip?

Lately only deadlines have been motivating me to get the next strip out on time and I have been missing a few. It's not that I am burned out in any way, it's that I have so many (mainly self-imposed) demands on my time. But in general, what motivates me to create entertainment is the larger question, I think. I think there are a lot more class clowns than grown-up humorists. It's easy to bust up your friends in front of the teacher, so you think you want to write when you go to college. I was one of those directionless slacker kids for the most part. I thought I could just "go into writing" and cruise on my natural talent.

Turns out there's an oversupply of smartasses. When you bump up against how hard it is to get someone to pay you for your alleged wit, most would-be writers face economic reality in short order. Short order, as in cook, as in flipping burgers is worth more than flippancy in U.S. dollars.

I personally was full of dreams and ambition and after about four years out of college was more or less empty of all that. I drifted into database programming, which was easy to learn and paid pretty well. Late in 2001, two things happened to rattle me. One, everybody knows about. The other was that a friend of mine died and I found myself speaking at his memorial. He was a talented illustrator. He and I were supposed to have been the creative team that set the world on fire. We tried to get two comic strips syndicated in the early '90s. And tried to sell two comic book series.

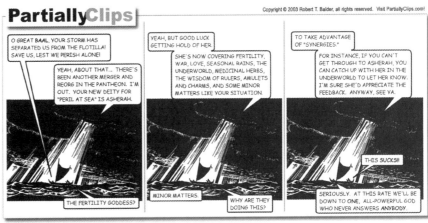

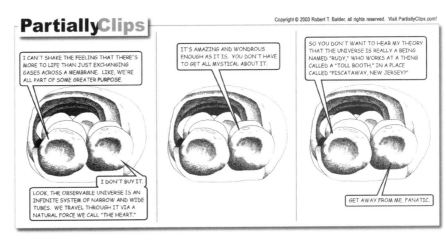

"Belch Burger," an early comic strip idea by Balder.

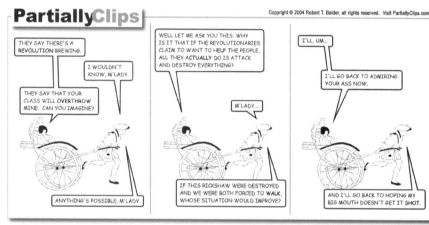

Struck out all around. At the memorial I was talking about all of the projects we did and wanted to do and I realized he was dead. None of that great stuff would ever get done by him now.

And the fact was, I could get creamed on the Beltway the next day and I wouldn't have done anything noteworthy with my dreams and talent, either. I'd have no creative legacy.

So I picked one abandoned project from the giant pile of abandoned projects and that was the clip art format comic strip. Could just as easily have been one of my novels or radio show or television show. I picked the most doable, and vowed to myself to see it through. I renamed it, researched webcomics and got myself a three-year plan to develop it into a business. But the short answer to all of that is, "fear of mortality" is what motivates me to keep going with the strip and the other creative projects I do. I have this great print I bought at a science fiction convention. It's a drawing of a human hand, reaching up. Only the fingers and thumb are all candles, burning down. I keep it over my computer and look at it sometimes when I know I am losing momentum. I've got a certain amount of time left, of unknown length, to do whatever I can do. To create whatever my hand can create.

What is the worst aspect of cartooning as a career? The best?

The worst aspect is probably the low value that society sets on what I do, in terms of monetary worth. I can deal with uncertainty and I can deal with the responsibility resting on me to make worthwhile content. Not that I'm not in favor of a free market, but it's a bit discouraging to think that on an hour-by-hour basis, I could make more money pumping out septic tanks.

The best thing about it is, of course, the freedom. (Self-expression, I mean, not just not having to clean out septic tanks.) A close second best is the amazing number of good people I have met who do comics.

Do you care if cultural arbiters take comics seriously?

Hm. Not really, no. If you mean the sort of literary cognoscenti who write book columns in mainstream dailies, then not at all. There are different kinds of cultural arbiters, though. There are those influences among us who make the herd decide what is cool. There are the decision makers at media conglomerates who decide what to shove in people's faces next year.

And then there are those of us who are just getting together and making culture by the weight of our collective personal free choices. I'm answering this question on my Blackberry at a science fiction convention. Within my sight are people dressed as belly dancers, a Star Wars rebel pilot, a Roman Centurion, and a nurse. We're enjoying the hell out of the culture we're creating. We don't need arbitration.

What kind of music do you listen to?

Geek rock, mostly. Hard to define, I guess. But rock with intelligent lyrics. They Might Be Giants is easily my favorite band. I had a choral background so I like stuff with tight vocal harmonies, too.

I'm also involved in what is called filk music. This is music for and by fans of Fantasy and Science Fiction. It has its own convention circuit and community. I wrote, performed, produced and manufactured my own CD, with another in production for Spring 2006. I frequently perform concerts at conventions. Filk is nearly as big a part of my creative life as comics, and I have similarly made many friends among the creative people in that community. A lot of the music I listen to is made by people I know.

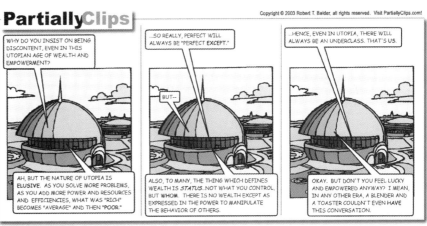

Chris Dlugosz

Wallowing in digitalia

When Chris Dlugosz was ten years old, he won first place in New York State's Invention Convention for small bendable flags to make parking spaces easier to find. By day a freelance graphic designer, at night he creates "Pixel"—arguably the webbiest of webcomics. Here's what a Belgian Web site has to say: "Chris Dlugosz (Wat een naam!) heeft er al een heel deel gemaakt, en hij toont ze op zijn Web site. Ik vond de bijgevoegde strip best wel grappig (even op klikken en dan wordt hij uitvergroot). Maar ja, het is er één van de vele andere, misschien vind ik straks een veel betere..." Chris is 25.

TED RALL: In "Pixel" the media is the message. You revel in the digitalized nature of webcomics, embracing fully what other cartoonists merely use as a delivery device for work that in days past might have just as easily appeared in print. What was your thinking when you began the strip?

CHRIS DLUGOSZ: At first, I started cranking out some "Pixel" strips as a casual gag, making fun of another genre of webcomics, called "sprite comics." Sprites are pixilated videogame characters and people love to use nostalgic Nintendo icons as their little webcomic characters. I was annoyed by the simplicity of sprite comics, so I decided to make fun of them by using talking squares, bluntly and inanely simple. The logistics of my "Pixel" universe were slowly forged

over the years as I continued improvising, or rather making up excuses for why things are the way they are. I went into this with no real plan and to this day I have no ultimate goal.

Which is probably best. Do you find yourself developing strips in order to give you an excuse to use some interesting visual effect?

Not particularly. I always begin with the writing and I do all of the text first because text has the annoying tendency to cover up much of your art. So I save art and decorative visuals for last. Interesting visual effects can almost be considered a side hobby of mine, one that happens to be included in my writing for "Pixel" now and then.

What are your aesthetic and/or cartooning influences?

I was most inspired to do a creative project by reading all of Bill Watterson's "Calvin & Hobbes," a comic that capitalizes on childhood follies and nostalgia, with facetious philosophy interwoven. This comic is the sole reason I was not afraid to occasionally get rhetorical or philosophical in some of my own strips.

Of course my aesthetics are very different from "Calvin & Hobbes," or from most other comics for that matter. I intentionally tried to keep the look of my strip far away from standard cartooning. There is more geometry than there is actual drawing. I try to make my strip into what I wish

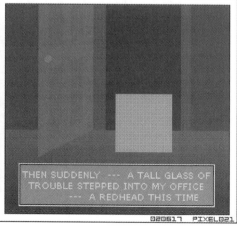

other comics would be. For example, I always do just three panels, because I am usually too lazy to read longer, full-page comics.

Another influence is the one that every webcomic author will tell you about: "Penny Arcade" is the one webcomic that got popular first, and is still going strong to this day. They introduced me to the concept of the webcomic.

The look is brittle and cold, the graphic equivalent of the German band Kraftwerk. Is that intentional?

I like that comparison. I make it look cold, stark, etc., because that is my personal taste. I celebrate precision, finding it beautiful in and of itself. I am a perfectionist. I very often spend too much time drawing single pixels for the finishing touches of my strips. This brittle outcome is not terribly relevant to the comic itself; it is just me. My main Web site, www.chrisdlugosz.net, looks similar.

Could you explain how you develop your strip from the germ of an idea to its final version?

My better strips are always the ideas that hit me spontaneously all at once, as opposed to toiling and brainstorming. I have a text file on my computer that is a list of new ideas for strips. If they are still funny tomorrow, I usually keep them in the list queued to be made into a strip later. Every strip begins with my template file, which consists of a red and

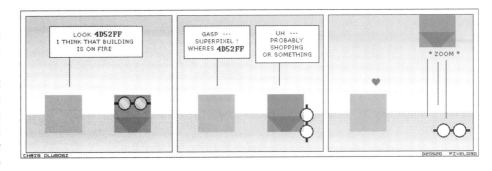

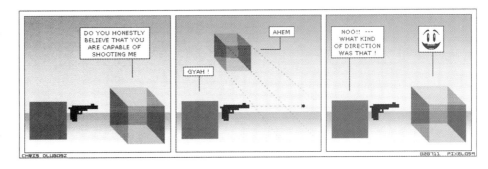

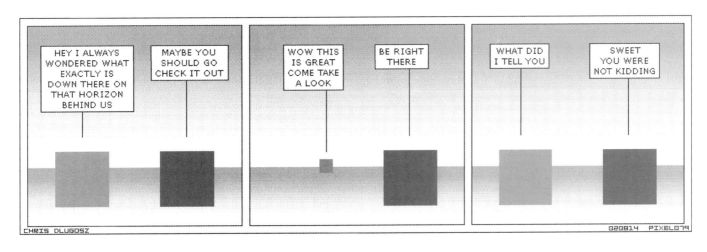

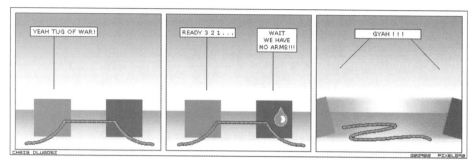

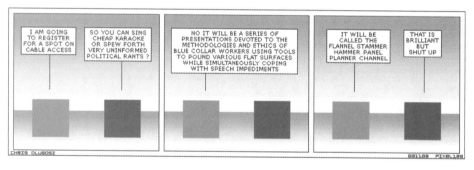

a blue pixel standing in front of a green horizon and blue sky. I almost always change the colors, to keep it all mixed up. I avoid having specific characters emerge. The meticulous perfectionist in me uses a random number generator to render two strings of six digits of hexadecimals, which I use as the color code for the pixels in the strip. Thus it is truly random. When the color is finished, I immediately get all of the dialogue typed up and enclosed in white boxes. From there, the look of the strip is dependent entirely on the events in the dialogue. If it calls for a change of scenery in panel three, then I do that. I keep every strip serialized and dated with the same dimensions, text style, and file format since day one.

That's amazing. And a little scary. Are you a super organized person?

I'm afraid I do revel in borderline obsessive-compulsive organization.

Yet there's also an anarchic sense of fun in your work, as in No. 213, wherein the judge's hammer comes smashing down in the final panel.

Certainly. That was a classic case of a spontaneous idea that got me to chuckle, whereas for many other strips, it was clear that I worked probably too hard on it. Nobody wants to read petty semantics constantly.

Knowing when to stop is hard. Sometimes the best cartoon results when an artist is faced with a tight deadline.

I have no deadline, because I do not publish anywhere nor do I make money. I am proud to have no annoying advertisements anywhere on my Web sites. The drawback of course is that I update with lackadaisical consistency.

Do your fans complain about that?

Once or twice. I suppose my excuse is that I employ quality over quantity. At the risk of sounding like a jerk, I think most webcomics highlight quantity.

Are you a futurist? Which would you choose to live in, the 16th or the 26th century?

I have no clue which time would make me happier. But I am certainly far more intrigued by the future, so I would choose to live there. I grew up as a child of science fiction, always bored with history. Only recently in college have such topics as ancient Roman culture become fascinating to me.

Morally speaking, I put myself in full support of certain controversial issues such as cloning and genetic engineering. My justification is that, no matter what we humans do, it is all still natural on this petri dish called earth, no different than beavers erecting dams.

But technical innovation doesn't always equal progress.

My stance on that issue can swivel depending on the mere current of my mood. Sometimes I consider progress to be the absorption of all knowledge

Early influence for Pixel? Playing with the music section of Mario Paint for Super Nintendo and "being a geek as always," said Dlugosz.

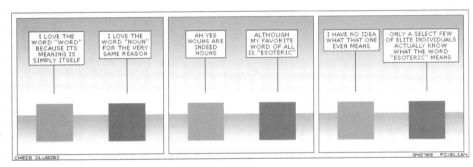

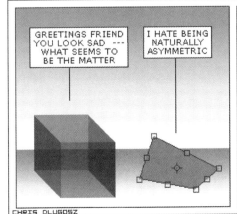
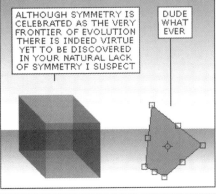

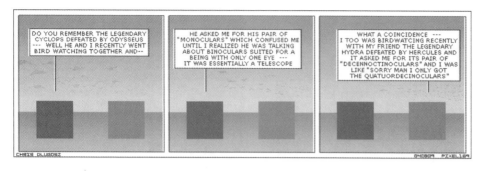

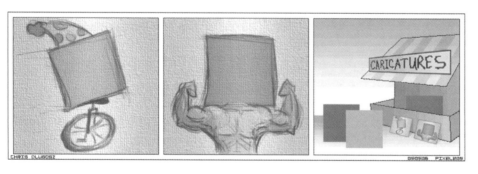

Dlugosz was a winner in the New York Invention Convention in 1992. His invention was flags in parking spaces that bend down when cars park over them, so empty spaces could be easily identified.

of ourselves and the universe, and other times I consider progress to be prevalence of our species. And of course those two ideals tend to conflict now and then.

You're obviously interested in identifiers, as when you explore naming characters/shapes as numbers rather than traditional names. Why?

That is probably another celebration of specificity. There is something about serialization that greatly appeals to me. Meanwhile, personal names are rarely important in my comic because I ended up focusing more on races/species/shapes.

I've asked this question of other artists in this book, but in your case it seems particularly relevant: would your work look as good in print?

Color is certainly very important in my comic, not necessarily meaningful, but just carefully chosen. The

definition of a pixel is an element that displays color for a picture. PICture + ELement = PIXEL. Black and white pixels are like black and white autumn scenery, perhaps. A good sixty percent of my strips would not translate well upon sacrificing color.

Clearly I headed into this project never expecting to get printed.

Beyond color, you use thin lines that are perhaps, well, one pixel wide. Paper leads to bleeding because it's porous. Has "Pixel" appeared on paper yet?

It has never appeared on paper as far as I know.

What do you want your readers to get from your strip?

I want people to get interested in pondering unexpected concepts, without me ending up sounding overly full of myself. And basically, I just love goofing around. I want to goof around with people's heads. I do not want people to pay me money.

Why not?

I have a strict rule in my mind that, all creative output is ruined or severely tainted the moment money is involved.

Because you start working to please others rather than yourself?

Yes. I am happy if others are pleased by work that I find pleasing to do.

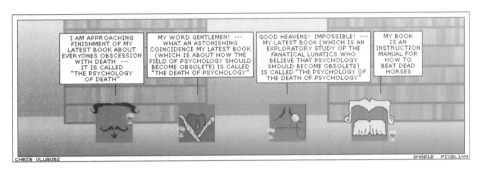

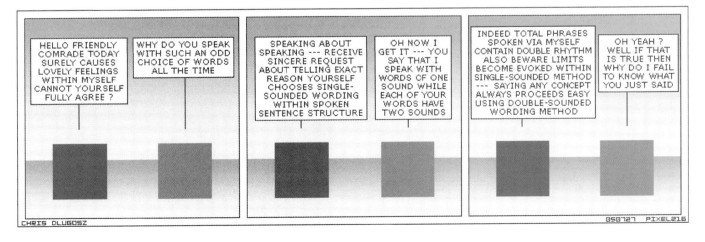

Adam Rust

Political commentary meets performance art in a scary place

Adam Rust's self-named Internet comic appears in the *Funny Times, Hustler Magazine, Los Angeles Journal, Hustler Humor Magazine, Z Magazine, Third Coast Press, Columbia Chronicle, Alter Magazine* as well as the Web sites lambiek.net, whitehousememos.com, preachintothechoir.com, mrwilliamsmagazine.com, getyourlifeon.com, gallopinginsanity.com, punchpanda.com, rottenzombie.com, and comicssherpa.com. A Wisconsinian-cum-Chicagoan, the 29-year-old Rust won a political cartoon contest at Columbia College in Chicago. He is currently illustrating a children's book called "The Middle School Student's Guide to Ruling the World." He has made installations and sculptures using dead woodchucks, dead pigs, cheese, peanut butter and jelly, dead mice and rats, sushi, fried and poached eggs and many other materials. He earned a couple of hundred bucks to create a battle scene using dead mice and rats in an alley. To get by when the dead animal gigs aren't coming in, he works as a "landscaper, carpenter, a lot of plain manual labor, a lot of chain-saw work, gardener, painter, art preparatory, mover, groundskeeper, nanny, whatever I can get, I take."

TED RALL: What is the "purpose" of "Adam's Rust"?

ADAM RUST: I guess at first it was just to be clever, and get attention, which I did. Then, it got more and more into social satire, and sometimes I started to have a message. Now, I try to be as funny and as profound as I can too. I guess what I've been trying to do, at least lately is to hold the public more responsible for all the dumb stuff that occurs in society. I feel less and less of a need to Bush bash, or complain that the Republicans are destroying America, blah, blah, blah…which is actually hard to do sometimes, because I so despise Bush. But, I figure that there are a lot of cartoonists out there throwing those punches for me. And they do a good job. I mean Bush makes it's so easy. I'm more interested in holding us, the citizens responsible. We elected him, we allow ourselves to be consumers and not people, we make ourselves obese (McDonald's doesn't force-feed us), we buy Hummers, we allow Paris Hilton to be a celebrity, we worship professional athletes, we adore Wal-Mart, we think NASCAR is cool, we allow the government to ship our jobs over-seas… the list goes on and on. I'm just tired of no one ever taking responsibility. We are so litigious in this country that it's absurd. I guess I still believe in freewill. So, I've been trying to shift more blame on the people in general, but be funny about it too.

Granted, not all my cartoons have some deep social commentary, some I'm just trying to be funny. But, nearly all of them are driven by pop-culture. And I think it's interesting that I am such a product of the consumer driven, media obsessed society.

So many cartoonists start as comics fans who hate what they read elsewhere and think they can do it better. Can you think of any specific examples of stuff you were specifically rebelling against?

The initial rebellion was stuff at the college newspapers, so nobody would know that stuff. But after I graduated and started my attempts to get printed elsewhere, I was really disgusted at all the mindless cutesy crap in the mainstream papers. I mean, I know these are obvious examples but stuff like "Love is...," "Curtis," "Hi and Lois," wholesome, family sap really started to piss me off. It seemed like it only spoke to fifty-year-old conservative white moms and dads. What about me, my generation? I read too. "Family Circus," I hate that too. "Garfield." "Cathy." Yuck!

Be careful. The art comix crowd thinks "Love Is...," "The Family Circus," "Nancy," etc., are brilliant, classic, awesome—in an ironic sense, of course. But you're not allowed to like "Cathy."

Hmmm, okay. I guess in a Thomas Kincaid, snow-covered cabin painting kind of kitschy way, I can appreciate it. Like a precious moments figurine. Or like a Jeff Koons sculpture. Oh, I'm just quoting. I think bad is just bad.

Except for Rudy Ray Moore's "Dolemite" movies.

Ha! I agree. But there does seem to be an embrace by hipsters to cherish all that is cheesy, which I guess I'm guilty of too. Especially when it comes to B-horror movies and stupid shit written on thrift store T-shirts.

Your best cartoons occur when you synthesize commentary on current American politics with pop culture, as in the cartoon about Disney characters where Aladdin meets his untimely demise at the Guantánamo Bay concentration camp. Does that intersection occur naturally in your head or is it something you work at?

I think that some of that stuff is really obvious, at least to me. But it is some-

Too bad we don't have color in this book ... A Rust-recreated battle scene using actual dead mice and rats.

NOW THAT JOHN ASHCROFT HAS RESIGNED AS ATTORNEY GENERAL, HE HAS AMPLE TIME TO PURSUE OTHER HOBBIES, PASSIONS AND INTERESTS, SUCH AS:

EAGLE WATCHING

Robin Red-Breast

Tufted Tit-Mouse

LOBBY TO CHANGE NAMES OF THE TUFTED TIT MOUSE AND THE ROBIN RED BREAST

REPORTING SUSPICIOUS PERSONS AND UNATTENDED PACKAGES AT AREA SHOPPING CENTER FOOD COURTS

PERFORMING EXORCISMS ON DEVILED EGGS

USEING BLACK MARKER TO CENSOR LEWD AND OBSCENE MATERIAL IN BACK ISSUES OF NATIONAL GEOGRAPHIC

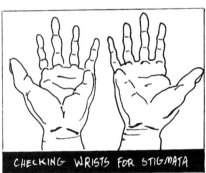

CHECKING WRISTS FOR STIGMATA

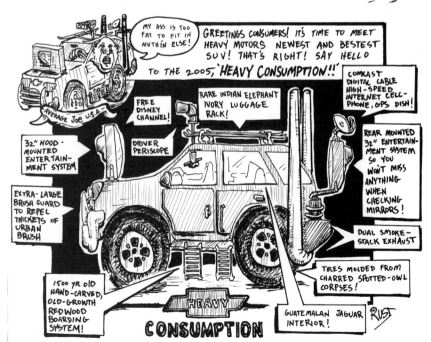

MY ASS IS TOO FAT TO FIT IN NUTHIN ELSE!

GREETINGS CONSUMERS! IT'S TIME TO MEET HEAVY MOTORS NEWEST AND BESTEST SUV! THAT'S RIGHT! SAY HELLO TO THE 2005, 'HEAVY CONSUMPTION'!!'

AVERAGE JOE U.S.A.

FREE DISNEY CHANNEL!

RARE INDIAN ELEPHANT IVORY LUGGAGE RACK!

COMCAST DIGITAL CABLE HIGH-SPEED INTERNET CELL-PHONE, GPS DISH!

32" HOOD-MOUNTED ENTERTAIN-MENT SYSTEM

DRIVER PERISCOPE

REAR MOUNTED 32" ENTERTAIN-MENT SYSTEM SO YOU WON'T MISS ANYTHING WHEN CHECKING MIRRORS!

EXTRA-LARGE BRUSH GUARD TO REPEL THICKETS OF URBAN BRUSH

DUAL SMOKE-STACK EXHAUST

1500 YR OLD HAND-CARVED, OLD-GROWTH REDWOOD BOARDING SYSTEM!

TIRES MOLDED FROM CHARRED SPOTTED-OWL CORPSES!

HEAVY CONSUMPTION

GUATEMALAN JAGUAR INTERIOR!

RUST

thing I definitely strive to do. It's good for me to use pop culture, because it sort of levels the playing field. It gives the readers and me a common ground. We all know who "The Little Mermaid" is. She lives in the ocean with a crab. So there are assumptions about pop culture already present and then that's less I have to explain. People relate better to it too because they're already familiar with these characters. They recognize them. They have a relationship already established. It really makes my job easier. I am both contemptuously repulsed and completely enthralled with pop culture. And thanks for the compliment.

You're the second *Attitude 3* cartoonist I've had to ask this to, but: Were you influenced by "Tom the Dancing Bug"? [*Attitude*]

Is it that obvious? [Ruben] Bolling is brilliant. Damn! I wish it wasn't that obvious.

It beats being influenced by "Nancy."

Word. I think he is amazing. And I love everything he does.

I always say this but that's because it's still true: he's the only cartoonist I consistently think is better than me, the only one whose ideas I'm always jealous of.

I remember in the first *Attitude* book when you said that. And yeah man, he's pretty freaking good. But don't worry, Ted. Your stuff is still awesome.

Your sense of humor can be cruel. Do people get angry with you? I'm thinking of the "uses for the useless" cartoon where you dress up the indigent as decorations.

Yeah. People get pissed at me a lot. Considering that comic alone, I got one e-mail that said they wished I would freeze to death under a bridge in Pittsburgh. Yikes! I've been protested in college. Students burned copies of the paper I was in, the *Badger Herald*.

That's awesome!

It was a joke about how stupid the KKK is and at the same time [ex-'60s radical right-wing pundit] David Horowitz had taken an ad out in the paper. My comic was shown on "Nightline" for that one.

It's also a little scary. Do you relish getting a reaction—nothing's worse than languishing in obscurity—or do you worry that someone's going to punch your lights out?

I love it. My parents think that. But I'm not too worried. I get into e-mail battles all the time. Any reaction is a good reaction. It means I'm reaching people.

Thanks for bringing that up. Do Internet-based comics spark more flame wars—rapid-fire insults and personal attacks—than cartoons based in print that merely happen to also appear online?

Well, during that whole thing in college with the KKK comic, then with a few others (one in particular about pedophile gay priests and another about a dog getting beheaded) a lot of letters to the editor were generated. On the Internet I definitely get mail. It used to be that it was angrier and there were fewer fans. But I think it's about equal now. What really pisses me off is that ninety-nine percent of the non-fan, threatening mail is sent to me anonymously. It just kills me that I'm hanging my politics and ideas and artwork out for all to see. Then someone disagrees and they can't even sign their name. Bunch of cowards hiding behind a computer screen. Not that I'm some kind of martyr or anything. It's easier for people to respond to you via the Internet.

No one's braver than a dude sitting in his underwear typing on the laptop in his parents' den.

For real. But, I got to say, I really admire this blogging phenomenon. It gives me hope that there is a new source to keep our media/"journalists" somewhat responsible. Even now CNN reports daily on the bloggers. I think that's funny.

It's undeniably exciting, but aren't you

Rust works on one of his installations, applying peanut butter to a Chicago street.

FATES OF DISNEY CHARACTERS IF THEY EXISTED IN CONTEMPORARY AMERICA...

THE LITTLE MERMAID IS STRANGLED IN COMMERCIAL TUNA NETS.

BAMBI DIES OF CHRONIC WASTING DISEASE IN NORTHERN WISCONSIN.

HI-HO, HI-HO, OUR WORK WENT OFF TO MEXICO....

THE SEVEN DWARFS ARE UNEMPLOYED VICTIMS OF CORPORATE DOWNSIZING AND OUTSOURCING.

OBVIOUSLY, PINOCCHIO IS A POLITICIAN.

AND ALADDIN IS DETAINED AT GUANTANAMO BAY.

A LOOK AT HOW THE INTERNET HAS RESHAPED THE HUMAN MALE PSYCHE...

—COMPUTERS SURE HAVE 'CHANGED MY MIND'.

worried about the unaccountability of bloggers? Right-wing bloggers helped bring down Dan Rather at CBS and a producer at CNN over allegations that eventually turned out to be untrue.

Show me a place where there is consistent credibility. I mean we have White House executives like [Bush deputy chief of staff] Karl Rove revealing CIA operatives. And then journalists with "integrity" like Robert Novak print it up. Yeah, bloggers aren't the answer. But I think they still do more of a service than a disservice. What ever happened to [disgraced right-wing White House correspondent] Jeff Gannon anyway? I thought Republicans were all about morals and values. So, how did a gay prostitute slip under their radar and become another one of their shills?

Just because a man rents himself out for cash doesn't make him a hooker. Wait, yes it does.
Where would you like to be, professionally and otherwise, in ten years? Twenty?

I just finished up my MFA this spring. I mean ideally, I want to draw my comics to support myself. But with the MFA, I could teach at a collegiate level. Which would be awesome. I just finished up this job as a Visual Art teacher to kids 7-15, and it was really fun.

I'll still be cartooning. Hopefully I'll be syndicated, or at least really out there. I don't necessarily think fame is my goal, but I like being a part of the dark-side of humor. Perhaps I'd like to see that relished a bit more, but then again, maybe I wouldn't be so attracted to it if it shifted more into the mainstream. It might loose it's appeal.

But, I think it'd be great to teach a few college classes. Then I could form my own little army. Really warp the minds of the youth. Reprogram them to serve as my minions.

But not surprisingly, I also strive for the good ol' fashion "America Dream." I really just want to do my thing, own a cabin in the woods, get a couple dogs, a shop/studio, and a hot-tub. Then I would kick-back and criticize all that see. HA!

Michael Zole

Testing the medium's limits via extreme minimalism

"**D**eath to the Extremist" by Michael Zole, a 25-year-old resident of southern Maine, is a continuing experiment in minimalism. Two quarter-circles talk to each other. He works as a UNIX systems administrator. A poster at the Webcomic Book Club wrote: "This is one of the best comics out there! I'm shocked it's not reviewed yet! With so many comics out there that fail at using minimalism correctly, this comic really excels in minimalism." That's about it.

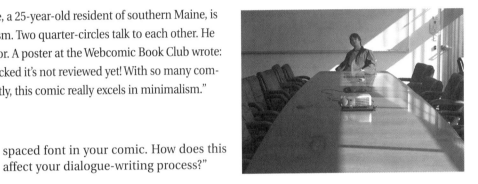

TED RALL: You have some "half-formulated ideas" for questions you wish someone would ask you. Please name one, then answer it.

MICHAEL ZOLE: "You use a large, monospaced font in your comic. How does this affect your dialogue-writing process?"

Now answer it.

I can fit about sixteen characters per line and five or six lines in a panel if only one of the characters is talking. I end up taking a lot of time with the vocabulary and phrasing. A cue I've taken from a lot of other comics, especially webcomics, is that you can get a lot of humor value out of unusual locution. So I've evolved a dialogue style that tends to be clipped and awkward. Long words are really hard to use. This might be the sort of thing I think about while writing the comics but that doesn't really come through in the finished product.

Now ask and answer one more of your own questions. I get the floor after that.

"Do your characters have distinct personalities?" If they do, it's not intentional.

"Death to the Extremist" ranks among the most minimalist webcomics, featuring as central characters two quarter-circles labeled "1" and "2." Is such simplicity of structure liberating or constricting?

It definitely limits what I can do. I'm perpetually jealous of comics with actual art, because they can pull off jokes and non-jokes that you can't do when you're repeating the same panel nine times. There's also a topical limitation, in that I feel pressured to talk about fairly abstract concepts since I'm dealing with abstract

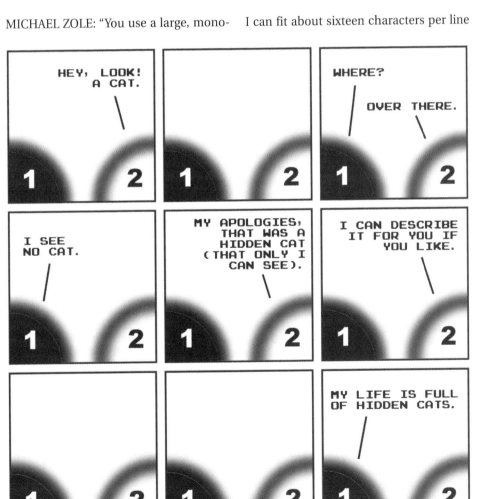

Comic strip panels:

PINK IS THE NEW BLACK. / NAVY BLUE IS THE NEW PINK. — 1 2

PLAID IS THE NEW NAVY BLUE. / STRIPES ARE THE NEW PLAID. — 1 2

STRIPERS ARE THE NEW STRIPES. / OTTERS ARE THE NEW STRIPERS. — 1 2

WELCOME BACK KOTTER IS THE NEW OTTERS. / I DISAGREE. — 1 2

SUSTAINED. / HARRY POTTER IS THE NEW OTTERS. — 1 2

NOT RHYMING IS THE NEW RHYMING. / NUMBERS ARE THE NEW WORDS. — 1 2

BEING HAPPY WITH WHAT WE HAVE IS THE NEW CHASING AFTER TRENDS. — 1 2

A NEW INVENTION HAS BEEN MADE BY ME. — 1 2

ITS A CHIP THAT INSURES YOU'RE ACTIONS ARE HONEST. — 1 2

PREVENTING THE WORLD FROM LYING, SOCIETY WILL BENEFIT FROM THE CHIP. — 1 2

NOW I NEED A TEST SUBJECT TO IMPLANT THE CHIP INTO. / HOW ABOUT ME? — 1 2

OKAY, HOLD STILL. / thok — 1 2

YOUR GRAMMAR IS A CRIME AGAINST THE ENGLISH LANGUAGE. — 1 2

I'M SERIOUS. THIS HAS BEEN BOTHERING ME FOR A LONG TIME. — 1 2

THIS CHIP IS GREAT! — 1 2

---

characters. So I get a little nervous that there's a finite number of things I can do with my template and eventually I'm going to run out. I'm kind of surprised that hasn't happened yet.

So why did you settle upon such a limiting structure?

Originally, I didn't have an intention to do a recurring comic strip. I was at Hampshire College, writing for the *Omen*, which was a student-run magazine that would pretty much print whatever people submitted that wasn't flagrantly libelous. There were a few other comics running, so I figured I'd try my hand. I'd had an idea for a theater of the absurd-type play, and I was learning Photoshop, so I decided to see if I could make a comic despite the fact that I couldn't really draw. I knew it was pretty basic, although it didn't really occur to me that I was being minimalist as such. I called it "Death To The Extremist" after that old contradiction "death to all extremists!". If I had known I was going to do more I would have called it something else.

Of course, you could have reacted to your inability to draw in other ways: taking drawing classes, collaborating with another artist.

Right, or just persistence. Matt Groening did several strips about how his artistic talent was the result of doodling throughout his entire education.

Do you think of "1" and "2" as interchangeable or do they have distinct personalities?

Early on I tried to alternate which one

Early digital influences for Zole: Nintendo at age 8 ...

... and on the computer at age 12.

of them had the first line in the comic, so back then, not really. I guess I tend to give One the lines that I might say, but I try not to put myself in the strip too much. I think it's funnier for them not to be identifiably human. And since they're not really representational anyway, there's nothing stopping me from casting them as famous people, inanimate objects, and so forth. Not long before the 2004 election I did a comic where Two was the ghost of Bill Hicks. It suggested that Bill Hicks, in death, had become ambivalent about politics. It probably wouldn't have occurred to me to do that if I had real characters.

The most consistent element is that they have an adversarial relationship, which is pretty common in strips that focus on two characters. At this point I'd say the important thing is the contrast between them, as opposed to having the same characteristics from strip to strip.

Just that there is a contrast?

Yeah, I tend to make one of them more myopic than the other and try to imagine the frustration that would result.

There are a lot of strips, and this probably says a lot about me, where one of them really wants the other's approval and the other either doesn't notice or doesn't care. It doesn't really matter which is which.

Although, to go back to the point about minimalism, one of the things about those strips is that I have no real way to represent the consequences of that. I can't show them having their hearts broken. I tend to just end the comic on a particularly cruel piece of dialogue and let the reader take it the rest of the way.

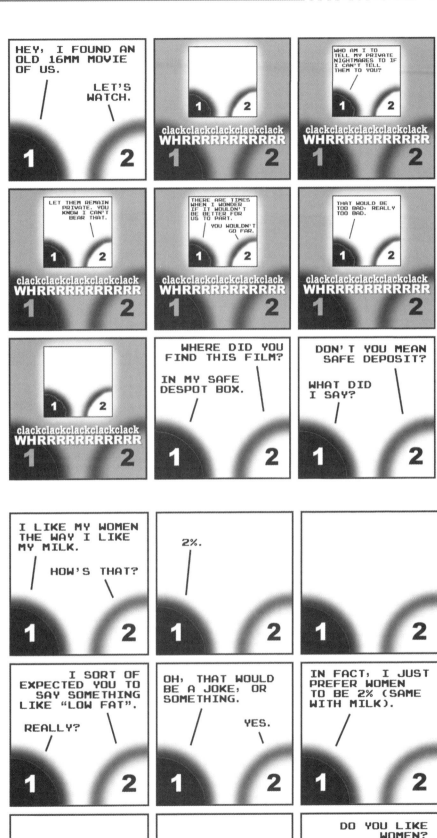

YOU DON'T KNOW MY NAME.
BUT IF YOU NEED TO REFER TO ME, YOU MAY USE THE NAME "MR. LITE BRITE".
YOUR SELF-CHOSEN TITLE SHOWS GREAT HUBRIS.
ACTUALLY THE TITLE WAS GIVEN TO ME BY THE ONE CALLED "DR. SIMON".
WAS HE GOOD AT SIMON?
OH, DON'T GET ME STARTED.
DOES THAT MEAN YOU ARE EQUALLY GOOD AT LITE BRITE?
YOU CAN'T BE "GOOD" AT LITE BRITE.
IT'S ABOUT SELF-EXPRESSION.

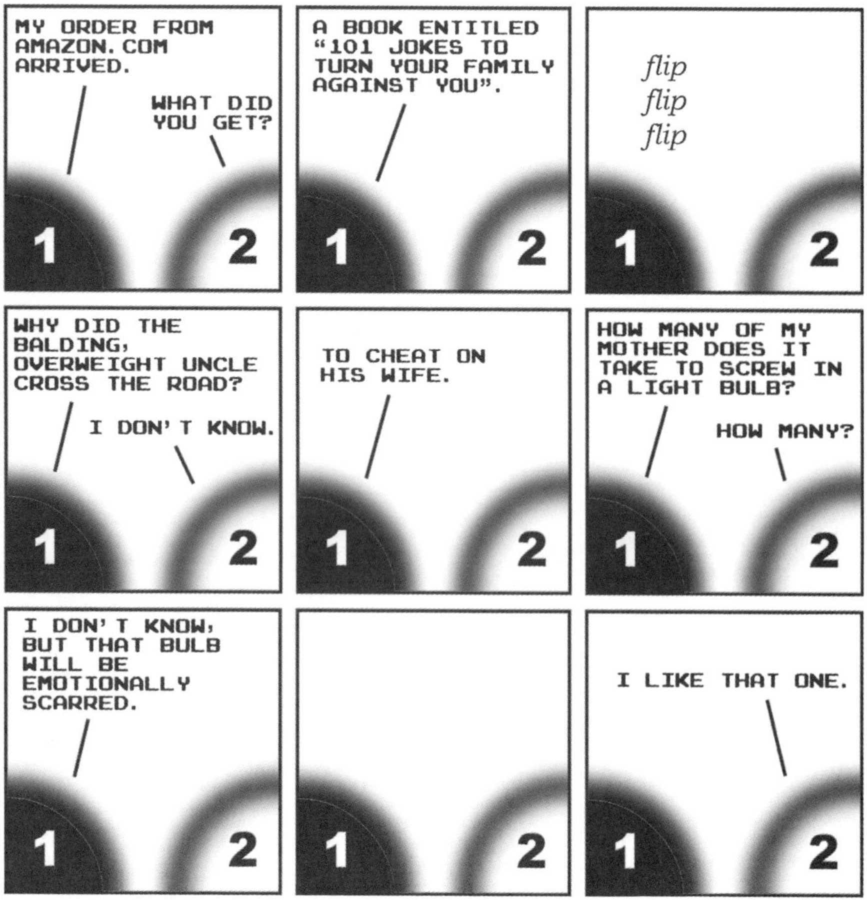
MY ORDER FROM AMAZON.COM ARRIVED.
WHAT DID YOU GET?
A BOOK ENTITLED "101 JOKES TO TURN YOUR FAMILY AGAINST YOU".
flip
flip
flip
WHY DID THE BALDING, OVERWEIGHT UNCLE CROSS THE ROAD?
I DON'T KNOW.
TO CHEAT ON HIS WIFE.
HOW MANY OF MY MOTHER DOES IT TAKE TO SCREW IN A LIGHT BULB?
HOW MANY?
I DON'T KNOW, BUT THAT BULB WILL BE EMOTIONALLY SCARRED.
I LIKE THAT ONE.

Conflict is the engine of drama, and thus interest.

Right. And for some reason I find that this structure I created almost by accident is really conducive to a more gray-area type of conflict, whereas a lot of comics out there boil down to one character openly hating another one, and that always struck me as weak.

There's a lot of rhyming in your strip. Do you rap?

A little! I'm trying to get into it. Rap fascinates me because it's both incredibly serious and incredibly silly, and often not intentionally, so it gets maybe a disproportionate share of the references in the strip. I have pretty standard traits for a shy nerd, so I'm not a natural rapper, but writing lyrics is a great challenge, and thanks to Keith Knight ["The K Chronicles," *Attitude 2*] I wouldn't even be the first person in comics to pick up a mic.

To what extent do you do this strip for yourself? For your readers?

I'd be lying if I said I did it entirely for myself, since if that was true I probably

Zole in front of some comics he drew at the "Festival of Creative Youth," a day camp he attended when he was 11. The comic strip was called "Mediocre Man."

wouldn't bother putting it online. But for the most part I'm aiming at my own sense of humor. You have to, I think, otherwise you're sacrificing the advantage of self-publishing.

Does minimalism ever spark hostility?

Not active hostility, but I think a lot of people are put off by the lack of artwork. I'm really divided on that, because on the one hand, it's not much to look at, and it's not inviting the way a nice, expressive cartoon character is. On the other hand, there are plenty of comics where the art isn't great but they get by on content.

The upshot of this is that I've never really considered myself a cartoonist in any way, and I'm still reluctant to call "Death To The Extremist" a comic. Although objectively it is, it just happens to be visually abstract. I've had an idea in the back of my mind to have someone draw characters to replace One and Two and keep writing the strip as normal, just for the sake of argument.

Would words typed into panels be a comic, even without characters? How about just characters that were shapes that were speechless and/or motionless?

At that point I think you have to leave it up to the artist. It may be stretching the definition of a comic, but that's how new and interesting forms get started. This may just be self-defense on my part, but even if it's not what we think of as a comic, it is what it is. My girlfriend is in a fine arts graduate program, so she's always telling me about different conceptual and performance artists and you really have to take their word for it. I guess at some point it's just up to context.

What's the stupidest thing anyone has ever said about "Death to the Extremist"?

A lot of people, when they see it for the first time, make a crack about the lack of artwork, as if I was trying to hide the fact that it's a template. I sometimes get e-mails from people who seem to be trying to imitate or reverse-engineer the way I write the strip, and their interpretations always seem really alien to me. I guess the perception is that I'm really trying to do something bizarre and unconventional, but I'm just trying to make strips that amuse me.

What is your least favorite comic strip and why?

I don't know if there's one I could single out. The

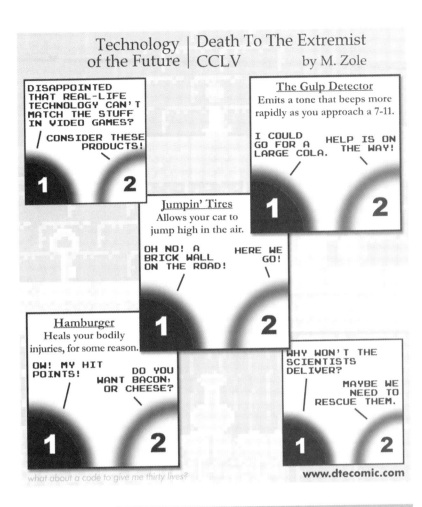

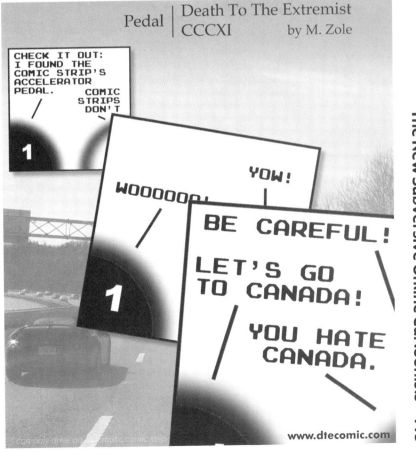

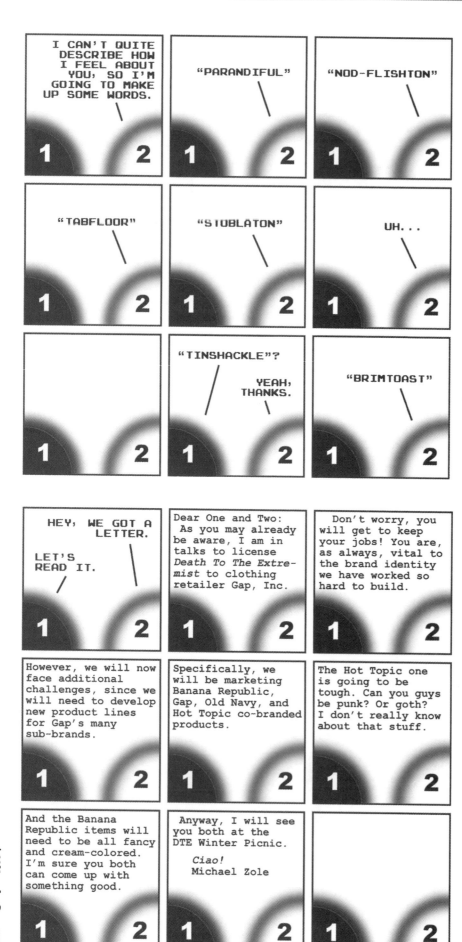

web is unfiltered by nature, so there's a lot of crap out there, but the crap doesn't bother me as much as the handful of comics that draw more readers than I think the material warrants. (I don't think any of them are in this book.) These comics always seem to have this quality to the writing where it's like they're desperate to win readers. They read like the script to a network sitcom, except those are heavily edited and filtered, so to see that kind of writing coming from an individual with no editorial constraints is kind of alarming to me.

I also hate comics where the art is sampled from old video games. They call them "sprite comics". I know I don't draw my strip either, but these comics seem to think that they're scoring humor points just by reusing old pixelated characters. I grew up playing Nintendo too, so I understand the nostalgia, but just because I get the reference doesn't mean it's funny.

How long do you foresee continuing to do "Death to the Extremist"?

I've thought about quitting, especially when I feel like I'm not having good ideas. But I think that's the effect of keeping a consistent schedule, and if I stopped I'd eventually start having ideas again, so then I'd feel silly. I think this is why a bunch of online comics have ended their run and then started it again. There's usually no paycheck to lose and plenty of free time to gain. So I guess I'll keep going until I feel like I've exhausted all the potential of 9 identical, featureless panels, but that'll be tough to judge because they didn't seem to have much potential to start with.

What's your favorite film?

I don't see that many movies, so I don't know if there's a single one I like enough to call it a favorite. I like Asian action films, and the occasional comedy that's actually funny. Actually, I've been really into documentaries lately, and there have been a lot of good ones. I like to watch "Startup.com" and be glad that I wasn't in the workforce during the dot-com boom, and "Dig!", which is like Spinal Tap except it's real and a total trainwreck.

Ryan North

Tyrannosaurus Rex: he's friendly, hungry and pithy!

Ryan North is a 26-year-old cartoonist who grew up in Osgoode, a small village outside Ottawa, in the province of Ontario, Canada, North America. "Daily Dinosaur Comics" features a fairy jolly-looking clip-art T. Rex and foils, almost always—like David Rees' "Get Your War On"—in identical poses. Emily Horne, whose "A Softer World" webcomic I unsuccessfully attempted to get into this book, writes about DDC: "Some people have written that think the visual repetition is a gimmick, or a gag. I guess I'm tempted to say that these people just aren't "getting it, but that's not really it. These people clearly aren't even *reading* it. Picture watching the same movie again and again, where the dialogue is changed so completely, and with so much skill that you forget that you've seen these images before. Now picture that every day for two years."

TED RALL: What cartooning work did you do before "Daily Dinosaur Comics"?

RYAN NORTH: Actually, I didn't do much that was professional! I'd do comics in class instead of taking notes, little one-page stories about people who smoked a cigarette which caused their eyes to expand and finally explode (this was a recurring theme, I don't know why), and ridiculous things like that. I remember going so far as to take scissors and a stapler into class and making little mini-comics on lined paper, distributing them to the people around me. I was a bad influence. But in my defense, I only did it in classes I understood so I wasn't falling behind, and I did it as discreetly as possible to avoid embarrassing my teachers. "Dinosaur Comics" is my first real attempt at a comic with a lifetime longer than a two-hour lecture.

There was one series before "Dinosaur Comics": an untitled series in which I would draw a comic on the first half of the page and do an over-the-top analysis of the same comic on the bottom half. It was fun but sort of a one-joke premise so I folded this into "Dinosaur Comics"—one of the earliest comics is about T-Rex analyzing his actions from a post-feminist perspective.

Where did you come across the clip art for DDC?

I had this program called "Arts and Letters" that came in one of those twelve-packs of CDs you used to be able to get when compact discs where new and exciting. It included some games and a CD of fonts, an atlas, things along those lines—basically all of the programs that Multimedia PCs were going to revolutionize. It also had this drawing program, which was not actually that great, but which did come with a whole bunch of clip art and with tons of sound

effects of airplanes for some reason. People at the time were still pretty confused about multimedia, I think. In any case, when I sat down to make the comic a decade later I didn't have Photoshop or anything like that, so I found this old CD and popped it in and went from there.

The clip art itself is actually pretty good, because it's arranged in pieces: there's a T-Rex arm, for instance, and a leg, and so on, which lets you put the dinosaurs in different poses than the ones they start in. So while the art for the comic is clipart, I did pose them a

little. Most of the poses are actually the defaults. I am not so much a visual artist. Shhh! It's a secret!

Are there many other dinosaur species available in clip art?

Yeah, there were! There's a Stegosaurus and Apatosaurus and so on—the ones that kids know, the popular ones. I chose the dinosaurs initially for their looks and not for their characteristics, but I ended up choosing, quite by accident, three archetypes. T-Rex is the most popular dinosaur, Utahraptor may have been the smartest (the species had the highest brain-to-body mass ratio), and Dromiceiomimus was probably the fastest. I have learnt a lot about dinosaurs since starting the comic.

Any pterodactyls?

Yeah, they've got pterodactyls! Are you planning to start your own clip art dinosaur comic? You should! You should also call it "Dinosaur Comics 2: Better Than

Dinosaur Comics."

It would be a great title but it might put strain on our relationship. I wouldn't want that. It's just that pterodactyls are my favorite. They fly! Well, probably. Now scientists say they aren't sure.

Man, scientists keep taking these awesome killer animals we've imagined for ourselves and making them more realistic! T-Rex is now supposed to be possibly a scavenger who walked perpendicular to the ground (not upright as I have him) and with feathers? I've been to a few feathered dinosaur exhibits and yeah, they do look more complete, but come on, we've already imagined dinosaurs as we wanted them. I love seeing the statues outside museums that were built in the '60s showing dinosaurs walking like we do and looking ferocious. It's pretty telling that that's how we first put their skeletons together.

Feathered T-Rexes aren't right. Too "Village People." Back to the comic:

dinosaur characters are a canny marketing choice, yes? I know I never tire of looking at them.

I think I got really lucky there. I chose dinosaurs because they looked the best but it could have just as easily been

Astronaut Comics! I'm lucky T-Rex has such a friendly face, such a willing smile that lets him get away with the stuff I put him through. Actually, for something that's lasted me three years, I really didn't put much thought into the original template. It could have been much more

terrible.

That's about a thousand cartoons. Do you plan to continue with the same format?

It's a little less than that since I don't put up comics on the weekend, but yeah, a good question. I was actually worried after the first month that it wouldn't be healthy to continue! I had this fear I'd start to think in terms of the "Dinosaur Comics" format, which has turned out to be pretty accurate, come to think of it.

I've always told people I'll keep doing the comics as long as they are exceedingly awesome. As soon as the comics start to be not so awesome I guess I'm going to have to try something else.

Has the Web version of the strip led to other projects, like freelance assignments?

A few. It's certainly gotten me a lot of offers for things along those lines, but I've, until very recently, also been a graduate student, so there just wasn't the time to do them all. But now that I've graduated, it's also let me do things like "Whispered Apologies," which is a spin-off comic I started in which artists send in comics without words and I get to write for them. It's a challenge, but also lots of fun and extremely flattering as well. I still can't get over the fact that people want me to write their comics.

It doesn't surprise me. You're a gifted writer. But do you get negative feedback from cartoon fans who think artwork is

more important than writing?

This has only happened about three times, I think. This surprised me, since not changing the pictures is a pretty aggressive aesthetic, and I was expecting more response. The negative response I do get usually this takes the form of arguing that since the pictures don't change, "Dinosaur Comics" "isn't really a comic"—which always struck me as a little odd. What else is it, then? It ends up coming down to whose definition of comic is better than whose, which isn't really that interesting a debate for me. What was unexpected about not changing the pictures is that over time the comic forms this great in-joke: the characters don't know that they're always in the same positions, but as soon as readers read more than one comic *they* do, and they're in on the gag.

Many strips that these critics would consider "real" comics don't feature much movement. "Garfield," for instance, looks pretty much the same every day.

A template that varies one percent is a comic. One that varies not at all isn't. Or so say the cartoon Nazis.

Yeah, "Garfield"'s a great example, since the illustration in that comic has decayed to the point where it's usual-ly just Garfield sitting on a countertop for three panels every day. But, poor Garfield! Everyone picks on Garfield just because it's a soulless zombie of a comic that's been telling the same jokes since the 1970s. But what I've found interest-ing is how much movement there actual-

Ryan North

ly is in a static template! You're not stuck with the same narrative: add a "YEARS LATER:" or "MEANWHILE:" and you can mix things up entirely.

Limitations in one area force creativity in others?

Yeah! Part of the fun is figuring out a way to tell the story I want to tell using these six panels with talking dinosaurs in them as atoms.

What are your long-term plans as a cartoonist?

Oh, God. I'm twenty-five years old, so Long-Term Plans have been a theme of late. I love writing and writing comics specifically and I'd like to do more like that. I've been talking to some artists on doing a serious collaboration, something long-term. On the other hand, it would be fun to write some non-comic books (I almost said "real books" there) too. There's writing in the future, at least, and hopefully a lot of that will take the form of comics!

A recent dromiceiomimus painting by North.

Steven L. Cloud

Bleak alienation comes in a pretty palette

32-year-old Steven L. Cloud's "Boy on a Stick and Slither" is one of the notable Big Hits of American webcomics. His sometimes tender, sometimes bitter and always beautifully rendered strip runs in print in *Esquire Magazine* and the *Atlanta-Journal Constitution*. Wikipedia sez: "Strips usually feature a short, pithy and sometimes surreal exchange between the title characters: the Boy who is literally only a head on a stick, despite which he is something of an idealist; and Slither the snake, who tends to be more of a skeptic. The strip is characterized by dry and cynical humor."

TED RALL: What are you trying to accomplish with "Boy on a Stick and Slither"?

STEVEN L. CLOUD: When I first began, I didn't have a specific goal other than to create a comic strip, but over time it's evolved into a vehicle for my own personal world view. I don't have everything (or maybe anything) figured out yet, but I keep trying, thinking and dreaming. Hopefully readers will absorb some of the content and maybe it will inspire them to think about the world in a different way. So, even though I didn't have a specific goal when I began, I think in the back of my mind I wanted to draw a comic that helped make the world a better place.

By making people think? Laugh? What?

Hopefully laugh first and think about it later. Most people expect a comic strip to amuse them. So I do try to amuse and entertain but I also want to stick some meaning in there somewhere. So maybe after they laugh it makes them think and consider the deeper meaning presented. I'm not saying all my comics tackle large and important issues. A lot of them are simply silly goofs, but I don't think I can maintain interest in drawing it if that's all I do.

Also, it seems to me that so many people stop learning after a certain age. I want to shake people out of this state. I'm well into my thirties now and I have even more desire for new ideas than I did in my twenties. A lot of people my age seem to accept things as they are and stop questioning. I think it's best to always question things. Especially the things you're most sure are true.

Cartooning is a war of attrition, one that claims many promising talents. What

Boy on a Stick and Slither present "Criticism"

From time to time...

I seriously examine and criticize my beliefs.

I may be wrong.

Because who knows?

Hmph.

It's cute how you believe in things.

©2004 Steven L. Cloud

motivates you to draw each week's cartoon? It's not the big money.

(laughter) Certainly not the money. This might sound trite, but I've always wanted to be a cartoonist. It's always appealed to me. Even before I could read I would stare at the comics in the newspaper. This isn't something I decided to do. It's something I have to do. It's almost like a compulsion. I don't make any money from my comic and I've been doing it for over six years. Even if I never earn a dime, I'll continue to draw it because it's so much fun. That's what it is. It's fun. It's not a chore at all.

How do you pay the bills?

I work in marketing, creating corporate Web sites and online marketing campaigns. I won't lie, though: I hope to one day be able to at least pay my bills with my cartoon. Working a day job is demoralizing. On the other hand, it's a great source of material for my strip.

Towards that goal, the strip runs in two print publications but its primary distribution is online. Do your Internet readers contribute money to keep it/you going?

Yes. Occasionally I get donations from particularly generous readers and I sell merchandise (T-shirts, buttons, stickers) through my online store. I'm always trying to figure out a way to make this work financially. There are other Web cartoonists who make their entire living from merchandise. I suppose that's what I'm working towards, but I don't enjoy marketing my comic as much as I enjoy drawing it. It's just a necessary evil.

I am trying to get into more print publications, but it's a very hard thing to do, especially if your work doesn't fit into an easily definable box.

You also break the mold compositionally, experimenting with panels, flows and backgrounds.

Yes. I trace that back to latter-day Sunday "Calvin & Hobbes." [Bill Watterson's] strips were very open and he used panels sporadically. I use the technique because

my characters stay in the exact same position every panel. I need to create some movement in the strip. The floating and constantly changing backgrounds give it a bit more life.

"Attitude 3" is printed in black and white, so people can't see the very pretty colors you use. Do you do a different black-and-white version for print media?

Yes I do. Color is a very important part of BOASAS. If it were up to me, it would always be printed in color. I know this isn't a realistic expectation so I will draw alternate black-and-white versions for publications. Printing in black-and-white changes the strips. I think they lose some of the emotional impact and childish, carefree attitude. Picking the colors of each strip is probably my favorite thing to do.

You use a simplified and stripped down style although it's clear you're capable of more detailed draughtsmanship. Why?

Because the comics I admire are the ones that use the least amount of lines to make a point. I enjoy simplicity. I think cartoons require simplicity given they are printed so small in newspapers and magazines. Granted, BOASAS is published online. I shouldn't be bound by that rule but I always wanted to strike a balance and at least give BOASAS a chance to exist in the print world.

What's the graphic and personality inspiration for each character?

The characters are graphically arbitrary. I was doodling in my sketchbook one day and drew the head of a boy that I thought looked pretty cool. I didn't want to mess it up with a poorly-drawn body so I drew a stick at the base of his head. Surprisingly, it worked. So I drew him and his equally simple friend. Slither exists because there's nothing easier to draw than a snake. The comic has always been a work in progress. I didn't know where I was going to end up but I knew I'd need at least two characters. Eventually the

characters developed optimistic (Boy on a Stick) and pessimistic (Slither) personalities. Essentially, the characters allow me to debate myself. They're the best and worst of me. I did want the characters to be iconic and easy to recognize. Kind of like "Peanuts."

As for the other characters in the strip, they play a very minor role. I think I created them for the purpose of helping me out when I was short on ideas, but they also help me be more directly political. For instance, The Florida Cracker allows

me to get certain things in the strip that Boy on a Stick and Slither wouldn't normally discuss. I grew up in northwest Florida. So it's okay for me to make fun of Southerners.

The secondary characters (The Florida Cracker and Frickles Mudcat) were especially useful during the 2004 Presidential election. I was so outraged over the state of things. My main characters don't discuss topical things. So, having a couple of other heads helped me be topical and political.

CREATING A MASTERPIECE - Jenni Helms seems to be sneaking a look at her competition while she and Steven Cloud engage in some creative painting during First Baptist Church's Vacation Bible School. They're two of the more than 120 students enrolled in Bible School at First Baptist this week, participating in Bible Study, Bible projects, and recreation. (And is that a spider on Jenni's finger?)

Early inspiration for "Boy on a Stick"? News clipping of Cloud painting at Vacation Bible School in 1978.

As Charles Schulz did, you draw a lot about the Big Questions: the (non)existence of God, the meaning of life, etc. What is it about the cartoon medium that makes such topics work?

These are issues people do not like to talk about openly. Try to bring up God or the meaning of life at most parties and watch people flee. Cartoons allow you to discuss them in a safe way. It's fun to hide behind the medium. If someone were to get offended by a comic I drew about God, I can always say "Geez, it's just a cartoon. What are you getting so worked up about?"

These are important issues to me. These are things I think about on a daily basis. I want to encourage others to think about them. The average person will not read a book on atheism or existentialism but they'll read a comic.

BOASAS is often set in bleak, desiccated environments—cactus, desert, hot sun. How come?

I grew up in Florida, but I've always loved desert landscapes and wide-open spaces. I've traveled through the Southwest and west Texas. The open space relaxes me and gives me a weird high. Maybe that's why desert scenes find their way into my comic. They're also very fun to draw.

Often the topic of my comic doesn't lend itself to a realistic location. Boy on a Stick and Slither would never find themselves at the post office or on a busy sidewalk. Their world has evolved into an alternate universe that's similar to reality, but not.

Most snakes live in jungles, though.

Snakes live all over the place. The desert, the sea, rivers, plains. I didn't want to have a specific setting for the comic because I knew I'd get bored drawing it. Ironically, I tend to default to the desert landscapes but this isn't set in stone. I can always do something different in the next strip.

Why do you think people like your strip?

I hope because it makes them think and because it covers topics other comics avoid. Maybe they like it because of the colors or because the characters are cute. I wanted to do something original. My influences are obvious but I try to be a little different. Whatever the reason, I'm just glad that anyone reads it at all. BOASAS is so much a part of my life, I'd be crushed if it was completely ignored.

Artist Info

Cartoonist contact information and bibliography

Rob Balder
www.partiallyclips.com
For Amusement Only (CD), 2006
*Suffering For My Clip Art: The Best of
  PartiallyClips*, 2005
Rich Fantasy Lives (CD), 2004
The Ball is Afraid: PartiallyClips Vol.1,
  2002

Matt Bors
www.mattbors.com
The Sluts of Guantánamo Bay, 2005
A Pamphlet For Torture Enthusiasts,
  2004

Steven L. Cloud
www.boasas.com

M.e. Cohen
www.HumorInk.com

Chris Dlugosz
www.pixelcomic.net

Thomas K. Dye
www.newshounds.com
Surgery in the Park, 2005
Regime Change, 2003
We All Came Out to Mantra, 2003
Press Badge Blues, 2001
Tonight's Top Story, 2000
Newshounds, 1999

Mark Fiore
www.markfiore.com
Mark Fiore's Animation Nation (DVD),
  2004

Dorothy Gambrell
www.catandgirl.com

Nicholas Gurewitch
www.pbfcomics.com

Dale Beran and David Hellman
www.alessonislearned.com

Brian McFadden
www.bigfatwhale.com
Big Fat Whale's Sea Anomie, 2005
*Big Fat Whale: The Lonely Captain's
  Erotic Scrimshaw*, 2003

Eric Millikin
www.fetusx.com

Ryan North
www.qwantz.com
Dinosaur Comics, 2006

August J. Pollak
www.xoverboard.com
*Monkeys Flinging Poo and Other Proud
  Moments in Media Punditry*, 2005
*Ridiculously Simple Graphs and Other
  Observations from XQUZYPHYR &
  Overboard*, 2004

Mark Poutenis
www.thinkingapeblues.com
*The Thinking Ape Blues Collected
  Atrocities Vol. 1: Out Where the Buses
  Don't Run*, 2003

Jason Pultz
www.scarybear.org
*Comic Strip Volume 1 : Scarybear and
  Friends*, 2006

Ted Rall
www.rall.com
America Gone Wild, 2006
*Generalissimo El Busho: Essays and
  Cartoons on the Bush Years*, 2004
Wake Up, You're Liberal!, 2004
*Attitude 2: The New Subversive
  Alternative Cartoonists* (editor), 2004
Gas War, 2003
*Attitude: The New Subversive Political
  Cartoonists* (editor), 2002
To Afghanistan and Back, 2002
Search and Destroy, 2001

2024, 2001
Revenge of the Latchkey Kids, 1998
My War With Brian, 1998
*Real Americans Admit: The Worst Thing
  I've Ever Done!*, 1996
All the Rules Have Changed, 1995
Waking Up in America, 1992

Adam Rust
www.comicssherpa.com/site/
  feature?uc_comic=cslbx

D.C. Simpson
www.ozyandmillie.org
www.idrewthis.org
I Drew This: Insert Title Here, 2006
Ozy and Millie VI: Tofu Knights, 2005
Ozy and Millie V: Om, 2003
*Ozy and Millie IV: Authentic Banana
  Dye*, 2002
Ozy and Millie III: Ink and White Space,
  2001
Ozy and Millie II: Never Mind Pants,
  2000
Ozy and Millie, 1999

Ben Smith
www.fightingwordscomics.com

Richard Stevens
www.dieselsweeties.com
Pocket Sweeties Volume One, 2005

J.P. Trostle
www.japenet.net
*Attack of the Political Cartoonists:
  Insights and Assaults from Today's
  Editorial Pages*, 2004

Michael Zole
www.dtecomic.com